WORKING WITH HIGH-RISK YOUTH

The Case of Curtis Jones

Alex A. G. Taub

Hamilton Books
A member of
The Rowman & Littlefield Publishing Group
Lanham · Boulder · New York · Toronto · Plymouth, UK

Copyright © 2011 by
Hamilton Books
4501 Forbes Boulevard
Suite 200
Lanham, Maryland 20706
Hamilton Books Acquisitions Department (301) 459-3366

Estover Road
Plymouth PL6 7PY
United Kingdom

Library of Congress Control Number: 2011926093
ISBN: 978-0-7618-5535-4 (paperback : alk. paper)
eISBN: 978-0-7618-5536-1

Dedication

This book is dedicated to the teachings of Anne and Clay Denman, who helped me develop from being just another confused freshman and taught me about life and anthropology.

Table of Contents

Acknowledgments

I would like to thank many people for the assistance they offered this project. Ms. Marilee Coscarart, Social Worker; Dr. Marcia Zack, School Counselor; Mr. John Nipps, Teacher; Ms Patricia L. Proebsting, Attorney at Law; Mr. William Homes, Director Of Juvenile Probation Department, Kittitas County; Amy Shank, Proofreader and all those who for personal, confidential, or professional reasons cannot be named, for their time and efforts to make this a much better work. I wish to also thank my numerous proofreaders, who each found just one more embarrassing mistake, that I hope was removed before publication.

Drs. Anne and Clayton Denman are my earliest mentors. They helped develop my interest in anthropology and scholarship. Dr. Clayton Denman was my first college instructor and took me under his wing. He trusted me as his teaching assistant and taught me how to succeed in college. Dr. Anne Denman then challenged me to work harder and do better. Together they encouraged my creativity, but challenged me to take the next steps to test my ideas in the real world. These teachers changed my life for the better.

Professor Tamsin L. Hekala was my graduate advisor, teacher, surrogate parent, tormentor and friend. She always pushed me to make my projects better and taught the ethic of success. She encouraged me to continue my work after leaving school and assisted me to contact other professionals. Finally, she assisted with the editing and development of arguments within this work.

Finally I need to thank my wife, Amanda. She permitted me to do field work with which she was not comfortable. She gave me the time to focus on the writing and encouraged me to stay on task. This work could not have been completed without her assistance and inspiration.

Preface

I started to write this book when I was working in juvenile detention. It soon became apparent that much of my college training was not appropriate for the reality of working with at-risk and high-risk youths. None of my classes taught me how to deal with potentially violent confrontations with manipulative individuals. An additional problem was that while many well-meaning people in different agencies were trying to help these youths, ignorance of others' efforts weakened everyone's work.

It is my hope that through this book, students who are thinking about working with either at-risk or high-risk youths will learn the following:
1) What different agencies do and how they work.
2) Some basic methods for dealing with difficult situations.
3) How their personality will affect which methods will work best for them.

The case study in this book focuses on life in a male juvenile detention home. The use of a group home setting is intentional, as it is one example of the unexpected jobs one might obtain starting out of college with a social science degree. Other types of entry level positions are case worker for a social service agency, classroom teacher, intern, or youth worker within juvenile detention. In most of these jobs the employee works directly with the clients, with occasional contacts from other service providers. By understanding the roles of these other providers, you will be better prepared to cooperate with them, and may open yourself up to other career advancement opportunities.

Since juvenile detention facilities are usually segregated by sex, and the author's experience comes from working in a male group home, this book deals with male youths. However, many of the techniques described are appropriate for working with either male or female clients. The purpose of this book is not to tell you how to deal with one type of youth or another, but rather, to help you learn about yourself, your biases and how they might affect your work.

The terms at-risk and high-risk to describe youths have been used interchangeable in the past; however, they do not mean the same thing. In this work I am focusing on youths who are currently displaying behaviors that are socially or legally deemed unacceptable. These youths will be defined as "high-risk." The term "at-risk" is reserved for youths who have a number of risk factors for displaying these undesirable behaviors, but are not yet doing so themselves. Therefore, this author has made a choice not to use these terms interchangeably.

The methodologies described in this book come from a variety of disciplines and theories. Different characters have different approaches which have been adapted to work with their personalities. *The main character's approach is to challenge the target youths to question the myths of gang life and to make them compare these myths to the reality they are living.* As the clients come to see the fallacies and weaknesses of the life they are leading, the social worker can provide them with alternatives to help them out of the gangs. The youths themselves have to choose to take advantage of these alternatives. Knowledge of other programs in your geographic area can provide positive alternatives to gang and/or destructive behavior when the clients are no longer under the direct control of your program.

However, the approach taken by the main character is just one approach. It will not work for all clients, youth workers or situations. Take advantage of your studies to learn a number of different approaches with which you can work. No one method will work with all kids. Remember, you will be working with a variety of young people with various needs and problems.

REVIEW OF LITERATURE

There are many fields which cover the various subjects covered in this book. What follows is not meant to be a complete list of the literature pertinent to working with either at-risk or high-risk clients, but rather a survey of the various fields which are involved in this work. Each field has many different methods to study gang kids, at-risk youths, controlling group dynamics, and leadership. The various strengths and weaknesses of these approaches are illustrated by an examination of the literature these fields produce.

Writings from the field of criminal justice tend to focus on the courts, crime and punishment. *The Children Savers: Juvenile Justice Observed* by Peter Prescott (1981) documents in a case study format the operations of a juvenile court system in a major city. The author did his research by observing the operations of the court, and concluded with a very negative view of the system. Because the author was only observing the system, and was not a participant, it is much harder for him to understand the situation in which the individuals in the system find themselves. *Folklore and Folklife in a Juvenile Corrections Institution,* by Davis Steven Cohen and John Eilertsen (1985), is a similar study where youths were observed and interviewed by the researchers. This method permitted the researchers to verify the answers in the interviews against the behaviors they observed. However, because they were only at the facility for a limited period of time, the youths would control what they say and how they behaved as the researchers would not have the opportunity to be trusted.

Comparing the Criminal Behavior of Youth Gangs and At-Risk Youths by C. Ronald Huff (1998) focused on youths in urban and suburban areas, looking at the similarities and differences of those at-risk youths who joined gangs and those who did not. Again, this study was based on brief interviews and statistical analysis. In the article "Describing and Defining Youth Gangs" by John Pitts (2008), the author analyzes how different authors have described youth gangs from a local situation, to their reach as international institutions of organized crime. This work can help readers to understand why so many different authors see these youth problems differently. All of these studies look specifically at the criminal behaviors, and not the factors which the youths experienced during their lives. These studies were limited by funding and time, and thus did not study changes in the target youths over time.

Sociology and psychology share many methods of research, but while sociology focuses on the actions of the society and larger groups, psychology studies the development of the individual and how the individual behaves when with others. *"Drinking, Kicking Back and Gang Banging": Alcohol, Violence and Street Gangs,* by Geoffrey Hunt, Karen Joe, and Dan Waldorf (1996) uses interviews and statistical analysis to examine the relationship between drinking and gang activities. The authors interviewed 658 gang members over a four-year period. This method permitted the researchers to achieve a detailed study focused on one point in these subjects' lives as part of gangs. *Old Heads Tell Their Stories; From Street Gangs to Street Organizations in New York City,* by Davis C. Brotherton (1997), is a mix of sociology's focus on the group behavior, while using psychology's lens of individual growth and development. The researcher examined the literature describing gang behaviors of the 1970s and 1980s. He then interviewed older members of the community who had been involved in gang behaviors during these periods. He found that they were still involved in these youth gangs, but now as adult role models, changing the youth affiliations from street gangs to street associations. By interviewing the older gang members he was able to verify the older research, and understand the changes that were taking place within a historical context.

Both sociology and psychology also have numerous texts in clinical counseling and social works, such as *Group Counseling and Psychotherapy with Adolescents,* by Beryce W. MacLennan and Naomi Felsenfeld (1968). This book addresses specific methods and theory of applied clinical work. Those who are actively working with at-risk clients should be familiar with a variety of these types of works, as they provide ideas for dealing with the various situations in which professionals can find themselves.

Research produced by the field of education most often focuses on the educational process. The educational process need not take place in a typical classroom, as is illustrated in *California Prison Gang Project, Final Report*, by Eric Cummins (1995). This article, written by an independent scholar, researches the educating of young gang members into gang culture during their time in prison. More typical education research often involves one teacher and the class with which they are working during a particular year. *Death at an Early Age*, by Jonathan Kozol (1967), while a dated example, still has many accurate and clear lessons to teach its readers, as many of the problems described by the author are still present today. This work is considered a classic and is often cited even 40 years later.

Another form of education research, often funded by either government or large organizations, focuses on the larger problems of at-risk youths and education. *Lessons from the Gang*, in *The School Administrator* by Beverly B. Reep (1996), is a study conducted by interviewing various gang members to collect their perception of what does and does not work for them in the modern education system. All of these articles and books focus on education, and look at the larger picture of the lives of at-risk youths, only to make further points about education. These studies are also limited to a set period of time and can only give the researcher a snapshot of the situation.

Anthropology does conduct studies where changes over time are observed by participants within the environment. *Chicano Prisoners: The Key to San Quentin* by R. Theodore Davidson (1974) is a study over the course of a year where the researcher was directly involved with his subjects during the whole of his study. Dr. Davidson interviewed his subjects, observed their behaviors, and was able to question both the staff of the prison and his subjects about what he was seeing during the year. He was able to observe how various groups of inmates use social control, peer pressure and pecking order to control the social environment. *Group Processes and Street Identity: Adolescent Chicano Gang Members* by James Diego Vigil (1988) is an article based on Dr. Vigil's extensive participant observation studies in the Los Angeles area. Again, this method permits the researcher to verify the interviews through long-term contact, and allows the researcher to earn the trust of their subjects. This trust allows the researcher to observe behavior the subjects do not want observed by an unknown outsider, such as specific criminal or drug activities. The long-term nature of the research also allows the researcher to observe changes in leadership within various gangs and how new members work their way into the gang. Unfortunately, this method limits the researcher to one specific geographic area and also limits the researcher's ability to perform cross-cultural comparisons. Anthropology research projects and specific methods are rarely prepared in cooperation with others in advance, so that statistics methods from one case study author are rarely comparable to those written by another.

It is becoming more common for researchers to use an interdisciplinary approach to avoid some of the problems listed above. *Long Engagements: Maturity in Modern Japan* by David W. Plath (Stanford, California, 1980) uses a triple-check methodology. First the researcher conducted interviews and collected stories during the course of his extended stay in Japan. His observations then served as a check against what he was being told during the interviews. Before publishing his work, Dr. Plath translated the work into Japanese and had his subjects review what he had written and observed. This allowed the subjects of his study to be a check against the researcher's own bias. *Estudio de una banda juvenil en una comunidad de alto riesgo: Resultados de la fase de iniciacion de la relación* in *Salud Mental* (1989) was the report of a research project undertaken by the Mexican Institute of Psychology. The researchers used a participant observation method, an anthropological approach, which permitted them to work with the subject population which might not be accessible using standard psychological methods. Because the researchers were in contact with their subjects in an environment which the subjects chose, they were able to gather behavioral data which would not have been revealed to them by using typical psychological approaches. However, while multidisciplinary approaches do allow the researcher to make new connections and understandings, the researcher is also removed from the specific details which working in only one field permits.

This book attempts to take advantage of each previously mentioned method's strengths. It takes the field ethnography of anthropology and, using the writing methods taught by Clifford Geertz (1973), attempts to allow the reader a more vivid mental picture of the environment. This author also used methods of writing described in *Writing Culture* (1986) to allow for the merging of actual events into a flowing story. This work has since been reviewed by numerous experts and former at-risk and high-risk youths, to make sure the events described are accurate. The strength of the fictive narrative was again argued by Andrew Beatty (2010) in *How Did It Feel for You? Emotion, Narrative and the Limits of Ethnography*, where the author concluded that the use of fictive voice rather than the objective voice, allows the reader a more persona understanding of the information. Based on this approach and to protect confidentiality of informants, all names have been changed or altered within the text. Different events have been combined, while others have been separated into different chapters.

However, there were some areas of research which were more difficult to perform. One example is in Chapter 2, where the percentages of families receiving various levels of state services are discussed. These numbers were presented during a mandatory training in risk assessment methods. To verify these numbers by finding state documentation or authorities within the state proved almost impossible. After placing over ten phone calls to various state employees, the author had been told that either a solid source for these numbers did not exist or that these numbers were not set out on a statewide basis. By examining the statistics required by the federal government, one knew that these numbers had to exist. Finally, the individual who had taught the seminar on risk assessment methods was contacted. She disclosed that these numbers were spread throughout various reports and that the numbers in these reports are not conformable to each other. Thus, without personal experience to verify the numbers, an outside researcher would not have been able to confidently use these percentages, which were commonly used within the field.

There are many books that have the stated purpose of teaching mentoring skills which will be needed by those that are considering working with high-risk youths. Most are directed toward business and political environments. Many hard-learned lessons in leadership can be found in the autobiographies of those a student has learned to respect. *My American Journey*, by General Colin Powell (Retired) with Joseph E. Persico (1995), is a clear example where a reader can learn from a great leader who had to overcome many personal obstacles to achieve the success he is known for today. *Iacocca, an Autobiography*, by Lee Iacocca with William Novak (1984), explains the leadership style of one engineer who not only led a successful business program from the beginning, but who then moved on to take over a failing program and turn it around. Both autobiographies have strong positive messages of leadership in difficult situations.

The one book which is *strongly recommended* is *The Art of War* by Sun Tzu, translated by Thomas Cleary (1988). Any translation is acceptable, but this version is particularly helpful in its discussion of the major points and how these points can be used in fields, other than war, where there is conflict. This book is not pro-war or conflict, but rather teaches the reader to win wars by predicting where conflicts will arise and how to avoid them. If a student is a pacifist or not comfortable with conflict, this book can teach methods not only to avoid conflict, but to turn the conflict back on the one with whom they are working. This book only takes about an hour to read, but a lifetime to master and understand. Each student should get a copy and read it often.

Another series of books which any educated person in any field dealing with high-risk clients should at least know about are those which contain the laws of their state. For example, in Washington State, the state publishes *The Revised Code of Washington* every two years, with a supplemental edition released on the odd-numbered years. This is a multiple-volume set which contains all of the laws passed by the legislature, and an index. To find a specific law, one must either have the numeric code or look in the index for the volume, chapter and page number where that law will be found. A student should practice finding laws in general areas of interest, before they are forced to locate a specific law for an assignment or for professional need. Most states now have these books available by online search.

Through this discussion of some of the literature currently available, it is hoped that the reader has gained an understanding of what fields, other than their own, are studying the area of at-risk and high-risk youths. It is also hoped that readers will find these other approaches of interest and might use them in their own work. This is not meant to be an all-inclusive survey of the available literature, or the brief descriptions completely true of all of the literature published by any given field. These are overviews to assist the reader in finding other materials of interest, in other fields which might not have occurred to the reader.

Student Introduction

This book focuses on a detention or group home. This type of environment controls the way the characters interact with their target youths. Because the youths are concerned with their reputation among their peers, the youths may not be comfortable talking to staff in a casual or friendly manner while their peers are watching. Youths may want to protect their "tough image." In the text of this book you may notice the group dialogues use a rough and disrespectful language. This is not because the youth workers do not respect their clients, but rather that workers are dealing with the youths' concern about their image among their peers. More friendly and respectful conversations are best held one-on-one, where other youths are not likely to listen. This is not the reality in all youth programs, but it is most likely in a juvenile home environment, such as the one used here.

Because no one's career or workday takes place in a vacuum, there is material on transportation issues, personal issues, and family life. These sections are meant to give students a realistic picture of how the type of work they are doing will affect such mundane things as commuting (very few first career youth workers drive cars which are less than ten years old), and how a long rough commute can, in turn, affect their day at work.

A youth worker's family also has an effect on and is affected by the work we do. This requires youth workers to find ways to keep their family both informed about their work and isolated from the work at the same time. As you are reading, think about how your family will react to you finding yourself in some of the situations described in this book. This should influence the type of job you take and how you will go about performing your duties.

All of the characters in this book are fictional. The events described are fiction but are based on actual events. The youth are based on a mixed collection of many of the actual youths with whom I have worked. None of the names used belong to any of the youths with whom I have worked. This is done to protect the identity of those with whom I have worked. In addition, fiction allows me to take lessons learned during over twenty years of experience in working with at-risk and high-risk youths, and place them in a story that covers only three months' time.

This book is written with a practical rather than theoretical approach. Since many youths have different needs, no one theoretical approach will solve all youths' various problems. This book does not explain or give formulas for how to work with all youths. It does give the reader a more realistic window on the reality of working with gang youths.

This book is written with a specific organization. The chapters start with a list of questions. The questions have no right or wrong answers, but are meant to measure your biases before you read the chapter. Review each question and quickly write down your answers. After you have read the chapter and discussed it in class, review these questions and your original answers. Also ask yourself how you would handle the situations presented. Would you do things differently? How and why? If your answers have changed, you have learned something.

The body of each chapter is a fictitious case study. This case study is meant to provide a realistic profile of one youth. These are situations in which you may find yourself as a teacher, youth counselor, case worker, or probation officer. Curtis Jones, the fictitious youth of these stories, is based on many different youths whom I have worked with as a teacher, youth worker, juvenile detention counselor and social worker.

After each chapter of the story, the situations will be explained or discussed. This material will not give you specific ways to deal with situations, but will give you questions to think about, and will present different ways of thinking about these issues.

The next section of each chapter summarizes the major points of the chapter. *Do not assume that just by reading the main points you will understand what the chapter is teaching.* The material in this book may seem intuitive or obvious on the surface, but it is the depth of your understanding of how these points will affect your work methods that will serve you in your career.

Each chapter has at least one suggested class activity. It may not be realistic to do each of these class activities within the quarter system, but as a student you should look at these activities and at least think about how you might deal with them. Remember, the point of these activities is to improve yourself and your skills. Even if an activity is not assigned in your class, it may help you prepare for something that may be assigned as part of your job.

The three major points which this book will try to present are essential understanding for any potential youth worker in any field. First, know yourself. If you are lying to yourself, these youths will know it. They are experts at being lied to and lying. Second, there is no one right answer to a given situation. Just as every youth worker will need different approaches to be comfortable and effective, different youths will require different approaches to work with them successfully. Finally, be prepared for youths not to want your help. You will need to find ways to work with them and not fight against them. These youths are used to people who say they want to help, only to have these "helpers" take advantage of them. Let the clients figure out that they want to work with you and how.

Open Letter to the Instructor

This book is designed to help students grow and prepare themselves for the reality of working in today's job market. This book does not, for the most part, contain testable empirical knowledge. The chapters are designed to help your students question their own beliefs and challenge them to adapt to the diverse environments in which they may find themselves.

This will make testing and grading more difficult. At the end of each chapter there is a list of major points. Test each student on the depth of their understanding of these points and how these points will affect them and their approach to a situation. Ask students to look at their own personalities and explain to you how the ideas of each chapter will affect them and their approach to their jobs. If a student can adapt to the employment situation in which they find themselves, they will have a better chance at surviving and being successful.

A WEEKLY SCHEDULE

The following is a recommended weekly schedule. Obviously it will have to be adapted to fit into how your class is scheduled, whether you are on the quarter or semester system, and on what day the class starts.

Monday, review the chapter and the introductory questions with the class. This will give you an idea who in your class has *not only* read the chapter, but who has taken the time to think about the material.

Tuesday, start one of the group activities. Many of these activities can be started in the class or may require students to work together on their own time.

Wednesday, you can either lecture or bring in a professional from one of the fields mentioned in the chapter. One week you might want a youth program director, a state social worker, or a police officer who works in gang activity prevention. Try to find at least one professional who has overcome gang membership in their own past. These professionals can address in a personal manner the approach they take to their job and how they see the relationship between their professions compared to others working with high-risk youths.

However, visiting professionals can also give a more personal picture of their career and how it affects them. Ask these professionals to be prepared not only to answer questions about what they do on the job and their training, but also how they, as an individual, deal with the stress of their job. The professionals can also explain how their jobs affect their relationships with their spouses and children. In addition, students should be asking these guests why they chose this job and how the professionals' attitudes toward their job have changed over the years.

Thursday, students should give group presentations. Most of the class activities have a presentation component. Try to make sure that each student has to lead at least one presentation during the term. A major part of being a successful youth worker is the self-confidence not only to speak your mind clearly, but also stand your ground when confronted. Youth workers must appear comfortable and effective when presenting information to groups of youths, the public, in staff meetings, and in formal court settings.

Friday can be used to complete any presentations, cover additional material or give examinations.

I wish you good luck, a good term and successful students.

Chapter 1
Face to Face

QUESTIONS TO THINK ABOUT AS YOU READ

1) What are my expectations when I get my first job? Work Conditions? Salary? Benefits? Coworkers? Advancement?

2) On what experiences or education are these expectations based? How realistic are these expectations?

3) How do I deal with confrontation? When are these good methods and when might they make a situation worse?

4) Where did I learn who I should respect in my community?

5) How well do I work when I don't have all of the information I would like? How do I act when I am being sworn at and confronted? How will this affect how I interact with this person in the future?

READING

"Yo dissin' me man!!! Yo fuckin' dissin' me!!!" This angry kid yelled in my face. It was seven-thirty in the morning, and I had a kid waving his arms four inches from my nose and his body language screamed at me that he was getting ready for a very physical fight.

"I am not 'dissin' you. I am only telling you to clean this bathroom again, but this time properly. I want you to go get the broom, and sweep the bathroom floor, and then mop it," I answered as calmly as someone could after being screamed at by a fifteen-year-old juvenile delinquent who was at least six inches taller than me. Curtis had been here before, and he knew the way our program worked. We both knew that he was just testing me, to see how much trouble he could cause without getting in trouble. However, I had only slept five short hours the night before and was not ready for this kind of confrontation this early in my day.

"No way man! You do it! Josh, you're the one who is paid to be here," my sarcastic "client" answered me. He then made a number of threatening gestures with his fists near my face and moved closer to try to unnerve me. I guessed that he hoped I would make the ultimate mistake and swing at him first.

If I had any better sense, it would have worked, but I was new and hopeful. I still wanted to believe I could make a difference with this youth, or at least not to lose this job. Since I had been working in this youth home for only one short month, I was still not sure how secure I was in a confrontation with our clients. I carefully tried to regain control of the situation. I took one physical step backwards, while not losing eye contact with my imposing assailant. This gave me a safer distance and yet did not make me look like I was cowering away. I then spoke to him in a controlled deep monotone (and tried desperately not to sound as nervous as I really was).

"You are right. I am paid. I am paid to help teach you to take care of yourself. It is not like I am asking you to clean the entire house by yourself."

The kid moved toward me again and raised his voice again, "I know responsibility man, and you ain't teaching me nothing! All you trying to do, is to keep from doing any work yo' self."

I stepped back again but kept my eyes closely focused on my verbal adversary, and lowered my voice even deeper, "I want you to please go get the mop and broom, and to please clean up the bathroom."

"No way man, you clean it and I'll watch you!"

The heat of my frustration was starting to move into my chest. "If you don't clean it now, you will lose your phone privileges for the rest of the morning," I promised.

"You can't threatin' me like that, man!"

Realizing that this was going nowhere, I made a decision to end this confrontation now, "Fine, you are on room restriction until 1400 hours and no phone all day."

My young inmate gave me a dirty look. He was clearly thinking about putting his fist into my face, but instead he turned on his heels and walked toward his room. He mumbled all sorts of threats and actions under his breath, but that was normal. I realized I had probably given him exactly what he had wanted in the first place, but at that moment I did not care. I did not want to play into his game of trying to control my emotions. I had sent him to his room to give us both some time to cool off.

While I had just started this job less than a month ago, I was already serving as the senior detention counselor on some shifts. I was hired to look after what I was told were twelve low- to medium-risk offenders at a residential home. This was supposed to be their second chance before being placed in a detention facility with the hard core offenders. However, I quickly learned from day one that there really aren't any true low-risk offenders and kids will get "in your face." It took me a few days, but I found what I thought was a good way to deal with it for me. Each staff member had a different approach to dealing with difficult kids, but we all knew that we needed to use methods with which we were comfortable. If you tried an approach you were not comfortable with, the kids could see through it and walk all over you.

On my way downstairs to the office, I asked one of the other kids to take care of the bathroom floor, in trade for one less chore later today. He complained about it, but jumped at the chance not to do the lunch dishes. With chores taken care of, I turned on the TV for the kids to vegetate in front of, and walked into the office. Watching TV probably would not help the other kids, but it would give me a few minutes to figure out what I was going to do with this Curtis Jones kid.

First, I tried to calm myself down. I sat down at my desk and picked up the comics from my coworker's paper and read each of them, twice. Only then did I go to the filing cabinet and locate Curtis's file. I started to look for what he had done to get him placed him here in the first place. Each resident came with one standard neon orange folder. These folders were supposed to tell us all about each youth; but more often, they only told us a name and when to release the client. These folders were hated by the staff as they were all marked confidential, but they usually lacked any really important personal information such as the kid's prior record, family life, or personality traits. Sometimes they did not even tell us what the kid had done to be placed in detention. It was even worse when the juvenile was serving time for a probation violation, because the folders would not tell us what the kid had done to end up on probation. At least this time they had given us a little more information than usual.

Curtis Jones was the oldest son of Natasha Jones. He had a younger brother, Luther, and a much younger sister, Angelie. His parents had never married, and his father left the family after the birth of his sister three years ago. His probation counselor blames many of his current problems on this lack of a strong permanent father figure. He was currently being held pending trial on a Theft One charge, accused of stealing a fancy cell phone and personal digital assistant.

"Pre-trials" were some of the worst kids to handle. They all claimed to be innocent and that they don't have to do anything you tell them because the judge had told them that they were "innocent until proven guilty." First, the judge tells the youth he is innocent, and has all of these rights, but then the judge tells the kid he does not want to release him because the kid can't be trusted. The judge must have looked at the youth's past record of not appearing for hearings, and decided that releasing this kid was not worth the risk. The youth would probably not appear for the next hearing and would only be apprehended on a new offense. However, holding the youth in detention only makes the kid even more rebellious against anyone in authority. Finally, these kids have no idea when they are actually going to get out, and usually when they are found guilty, they have already served their entire sentence.

Then I hit the jackpot. I actually found his offense history. In addition to the current charge, this kid had already been convicted on at least five other offenses in the past three years. And I knew in the back of my mind that these were only the charges where he was caught and prosecuted. Clearly, I was not impressed with this youth's past.

After I had read what little information his file contained, I went to find my senior coworker. I wanted to speak with Mike about his thoughts on Curtis Jones before I went upstairs to face him again. Mike had been working at the house for only five months, but I liked the way that he worked with the kids. He came from a background similar to many of our clients, and he understood most of them. His four years of experience working as a military policeman in the U.S. Air Force did not hurt either. I wanted his advice, not only because he was in charge, but because I needed a confidence boost.

"Curtis's mother cares, but he is hangin' with the wrong crowd. If he did not hang out with gang members, he would not even be here. If you are with him one-on-one, he is O.K., and can even be honest with yah, but only when he thinks it's in his best interest. It is only when he is around everyone else that his temper and his mouth get him in trouble. For some reason he thinks he gets respect from the other kids when they see him 'going off' or acting crazy," Mike told me. "When you go upstairs, be patient. Forget the chores, let it pass. Let him decide for himself that he can trust you. Don't tell him anything. Let him figure you out for himself."

Reassured with this advice and a few minutes to lower my blood pressure, I felt ready to make another try at it. Back upstairs, I took in a deep breath, took the cold metal door knob in my hand and walked into the room. I suppose I should have knocked first, but it was too late now.

Mr. Jones was sitting on his bed, moping, and looking out his window. He did not even look up when I opened the door. He was a proud African-American, fifteen years old, with a few roughly done tattoos on his arms. On his knuckles were the letters of his gang affiliation. His face was still unmarked, but his dark eyes were piercing out into the distance. They were sunk into his face, as if to say that they had seen too much.

"What the fuck do you want?!" he challenged.

"I came up to talk with ya," I said in a forced slow calm voice.

"What the hell about?" he shot back.

"I want to talk to you about why you are here, and why you keep coming back."

"I am here because you told me to go to my room, asshole!" he shot back.

"I know why you are in your room. Why are you here in detention?" I asked, hoping to get the conversation on track, rather than just being shouted at.

"I'm here because some cop was a racist pig, and said that the cell phone I was carrying was stolen. He said that if I could not prove it was mine, he was goin' to take me in."

"What did you tell him?"

"I told him that it was mine, and that all my homies knew it was mine. He didn't even listen to them. He just told me I was under arrest, slammed me face first into a wall and started to read me my rights, while another racist cop grabbed me from behind and cuffed me right in front of my friends. It was bad enough that he lied to arrest me, but he just had to do it in front of my homies. That was unreal! If my hands weren't cuffed, I would have taken that pig down right there. They didn't even give me a chance to explain myself. They just said that they knew it was stolen and that they would prove I was lying later. They had no reason to stop me, man. They just wanted to harass me, and then they called me a liar in front of my homies. They are always stopping us and asking us questions that are none of their business. But why do you care?"

"Who says I do care?" I asked, trying to make it sound like I did not. "Did you tell the officers what you thought of their actions?"

"I told him man…and I told him what I thought of his bigoted ass. I told him that he could take his racist attitude and shove it up his white ass sideways. Then his homie grabbed the cuffs to make them even tighter and pushed my face even harder into the brick wall. They had no right even to stop me, man, and then he took me to jail. He's just a racist ass."

I was beginning to see that this was going to be a very hard pre-trial detention. He was still denying any responsibility for his being detained and would not even admit that he was holding stolen property when he was arrested. I realized that this was partially out of self-protection, as there is no way he is going to admit to a stranger his involvement in any crime before he went to trial. For all he knew, if he told me anything, I would turn him in for it. To be honest, given how he had treated me earlier that day, I just might. However, his voice and body language made it clear that he was not yet ready to consider or admit that he might be partially responsible for his own incarceration. But this was not the time to start pushing the point. Curtis would first have to learn for himself who I was and if he could trust me.

I probably should have corrected Curtis's foul language and reminded him that he should not swear in the house; however, this was not the time. I was just going to let him vent for now. I wanted him to get rid of the anger now, or this was going to be a very hard time for both of us. It was going to take some time before I was going to get him to admit anything to me, let alone that he had anything to do with the stolen PDA. We both knew that it was not his, but it would not profit me to force his hand here and now.

It was not my job to get Curtis to admit his guilt of the charged crime. However, it was my job to work with Curtis, discover his needs and interests, and try to get him connected with other community agencies that might help him stay out of detention after his release. But before I could help Curtis stay out of detention, I needed to get him to understand how and why he kept getting in detention in the first place.

I took a moment to examine my young client. He was sitting on his bed with his arms around his knees, and his head turned away from me, so he could look out the window. His room was clean, not because he was a neat person, but because he had few possessions with which to clutter it. I knew that his mother came and visited him last night, but she did not bring him anything. She wanted him to have a hard time here, in the hope that he would not want to come back again. From more senior staff, I had learned that the last time Curtis was here she came three nights in a row, and each time asked the staff if her son had been well behaved. If she was told no, she would ask for specific details, but my seniors told me how they could hear her as she told Curtis how these behaviors were not acceptable for any son of hers. If she was told that he had been well behaved, she would make sure to praise him, but not embarrass him in front of the other kids. In either case, Curtis would not pay attention to one word his mother said. To him, she was not a man; she could not understand his reality.

Actually it was rare for a parent to visit as often as Natasha. Most parents only visited once a week at most. Often when they came, it was because their kids had called and asked for money for the phone or for when the staff ordered pizza. The kids never wanted their homies to actually see them with their parents, especially if their mother or father hugged or kissed them. These kids thought they were men, and did not want to look like wimps in front of their peers. They just had to keep their hard shell showing; but like most eggs, behind these kids' hard brittle shell was a soft interior.

We knew that Natasha was a mother who really cared about her son's future. Most parents cared, but they had either no idea or no time to deal with their children. Ms. Natasha Jones needed to work a full-time job that paid even less money than mine did, and when she finally got home, she was usually too tired to deal with all three of her children. She needed a mature Curtis to help look after his younger siblings and help out. But, when he finally was old enough to babysit his siblings, his homies started to take him away from her. It was very hard for her to deal with the situation, and now she was starting to see these same behaviors develop in her middle child, Luther, and it scared her. Here on this bed sat the cause of much of her stress: a young man who wanted to blame all his troubles on others, including me, the police, and even his own mother.

It was hard for me to have sympathy for him. We both knew that he was guilty of possessing a stolen cell phone. We both knew he would deny it until it was to his advantage to change his story. We both knew that he had no feelings toward the original owner of the cell phone. I guessed that he probably helped steal the PDA in the first place. Yet here I was, trying not to express my own hostility toward this kid. Not so that I could learn to like him, but so that I would be able to work with him. I just reminded myself that I was trying to earn his respect, not his friendship.

My first goal was not to "save" this kid. Only he could do that for himself. I could only provide him with opportunities; he had to decide to change himself, and put forward the effort. All I could do was try to talk with him and hope that we both would choose to listen to each other.

"Why do you think the officer wanted to harass you and your friends?" I inquired.

"I told you man, the pig was a racist son of a bitch," Curtis swore without any effort or thought.

"Watch your language," I quickly responded. I probably should not have been so abrupt; however, the way he was speaking was getting under my skin.

"They are always stopping me whenever they see a group of my homies on the street. They always pull us over and frisk us. I think they got to be gay or something. I bet that the cops don't do that in white 'hoods.' But in the black 'hoods', we're all guilty of doin' somethin', and it is the cops' job to harass us until they can find it. Then they just arrest us, and lock us all up. If we try to defend ourselves, then they get mean," Curtis exclaimed, in a speech that I had already heard, almost word for word, from many of our clients. At times I believed that these kids actually all memorized the same script and practiced it together, from the number of times I had heard it in the past month.

"Were you or your homies doing anything that might have attracted the officer's attention?" I asked.

"Hell!. . . I mean, heck no," Curtis corrected himself. "We were just standin' there, hangin' out, and talkin'. There's not much more for us to do at night."

I noticed that Curtis was starting to be careful what language he used. During my first few days, I learned that many of the boys use better language when they think they are convincing you that they were in the right. I knew this was only a game, but I was playing along with it, since it helped to calm Curtis down. Eventually all I had to do was raise an eyebrow, and these kids would realize that they had sworn or said something inappropriate, and they would correct their own language before I even needed to say anything.

Curtis was actually starting to calm down. His breathing was more controlled and his body language showed less frustration. He was starting to talk to me, rather than screaming at the wall. His open flow of sentences made it clear that he was starting to talk more freely. This was not to say that he trusted me or was telling me the truth, but at least he was starting to try to work with me.

"Curtis?" I asked. "I am curious about why you keep showing up here. Not because I think I can 'turn you from the evil of your ways,' but because I am curious. I see your mother came to visit you. I know that she cares. So tell me, why do you keep getting in trouble?"

His answer was short. "It's not like I go out looking for trouble. It just always finds me." I realized that without prying a little bit, I would probably only get the street equivalent to the corporate line.

"There must be more to it than that?" I asked.

"Honest man, I have always had trouble find me; even when I *was* in school."

"I find that hard to believe," I commented. What I actually found hard to believe was that I was having a rational conversation with the same gang-banger who thirty minutes ago was threatening to use my head for boxing practice. This was not the first time I had seen such dramatic changes in the mood of the kid with whom I was working. Many of these kids have learned to change their displayed excess emotions like turning on or off a light. This makes it difficult to tell when he was acting or showing his true emotions. However, I have also seen this same quick emotion change in some of my fellow staff members when dealing with particularly difficult clients. So Curtis's emotional quick-change act did not really surprise me.

"Man, listen to me! You have no idea what my life is like, and you probably never will." I could hear Curtis's voice rising again.

"I am listening to you, and I do want to hear what you have to say, but first

I have to go tell Mike where I am and what I am doing. I will be right back. . . ."

Once again I wanted to take a few moments to regather my thoughts. This had changed from a confrontational argument to professional discussion, and I needed to take a moment to think about how this would change my approach to this kid. I needed a few minutes to think about how I needed to change my body language, voice control and attitude toward working with Curtis. I also wanted to let Mike know that the situation was improving.

After informing Mike of my progress and that we were both still alive upstairs, I went back to Curtis's room. His attitude had changed for the worse. "What do you want, white man?"

"I want to finish our conversation. I believe you were about to tell me a little about yourself," I said as I pulled a plastic chair up next to his bed.

"I'm not going to tell you nothin'," Curtis shot back, and turned his back on me again to look out the window at the recently leafless tree.

For a moment Curtis and I both watched the tree outside his window move slightly in the breeze. "O.K. then I'll just leave you alone." I got up to leave, and as I was about to close the door, I heard Curtis ask, "How long am I going to be here?"

Calmly I explained, "With your current attitude, it could be quite a few more hours," I answered.

"Hold up man, I was just checkin' you out."

I stopped walking out and turned around. I had actually expected this quick change. Curtis was just testing to see how much effort it would take to make me angry or if I took myself too seriously. It was going to take him a long time to learn to trust me, and this was just one of many little tests Curtis would use to learn what I was really like. Curtis would probably use many more little tests before he would say anything to me that he feared could actually be used against him in courts or on the streets.

"What'cha want to know?"

"Why are you here?"

"Because some racist cop . . . ."

". . .accused you of having a stolen PDA," I chimed in. "No, I believe you were about to tell me about how trouble always finds you. What do you mean always? How can trouble *ALWAYS* find you?"

"It's true man. Even when I was a little kid, I always found trouble."

"What kind of trouble 'found you' when you were six?" I asked.

"Man, you don't know a thing about life on the streets, do you?" Curtis asked.

"Well, as a matter of fact, I don't," I said. I knew that I was giving Curtis an opening that could be abused, but I wanted to give him a chance to either take this opportunity to use it or abuse it. I had just admitted my own ignorance of street life. Not that both Curtis and I did not already know how ignorant I was. It was obvious to everyone that I was white, middle-class, and overeducated. But by admitting this, I had given Curtis a possible tool in any future argument. Now I could see what type of person Curtis was going to be. Would he ridicule me, or try to educate me about what he believed his life was really like?

"Man, I had better tell you what you don't know, or you will never make it here in detention," he said, pointing out the window. "Man, you just walk out on that street and trouble will find you. When I was six, I would be sitting out on the stairs in front of my house. I was hangin' with some of my homies. We were sitting there talking about stuff we saw and things we knew. We was not bothering anyone until a cop come over and started to harass us."

"What do you mean, 'harass us'?" I asked.

"Man, he'd come over and started asking us if we'd seen who just run by us. We told him that we weren't going to tell him nothing and besides, we saw nothing. The cop started to get angry with us and threatened to arrest us if we did not tell him what he wanted to know and now. He went off and made all sorts of threats about takin' us down to the cop shop for getting in his way. We just ignored him, man, because we did not know anything. He then called in more cops and we all got taken down to the cop shop to be harassed for three hours. They kept callin' us names and tellin' us we was stupid. This was the same cop they sent to our school to try and tell us he was our friend, and here he was insultin' me and my homies.

"We sat in jail for hours until our mothers came and got us. My mom was pissed. She let me have it about my behavior and how we should treat police with more respect. She went off about how she had to leave work and almost got fired, just so she could come and get me. The way we saw it, we had done nothin' wrong. We was treated like dirt and disrespected, and even our own mothers took their side and we got in trouble just for sittin' on my front stairs talkin' to friends."

"Why didn't you just tell him that you did not know anything and leave it at that?" I asked.

"He would not have listened to us, man. All he wanted to do was bring someone in for something. He did not care what for, or even if that person had actually done anything. I mean if he had just kept running past us he might have actually caught the guy he was looking for in the first place, man. The kid was only a block ahead of him."

I interrupted Curtis's whine. "I cannot explain what the officer was doing. I am not in his place and I do not know what he was thinking. But what if you had known about the people the officer was asking about? Would you have told him what he wanted to know?"

"Hell no! What type of *dog* do I look like? If I had info like that, I would not turn my own homies in to the cops."

"How do you know that the people the officer was looking for were your own home-boys?"

"Man, I knew who he was looking for and why, but I am not going to turn my own homies into those pigs. I don't care what they did. And if I had turned them in, man, they would have killed me. When you live on the streets you have to follow the street's rules, not the cops'. Cops don't live with you; they don't follow you every day. But on the streets, you turn on someone and it will only be a few hours before they are out and looking for you."

I noticed that his story had changed, but I was not going to point it out just yet.

I interrupted. "Let me ask you this . . . was there any adult you could turn to when you were younger?"

"No man, you've got to be kidding. No adult can understand what it's like on the streets."

"What about your mother? She seems very concerned about what's going on in your life."

"Man, she done nothin'. All she does is work all day and sometimes all night. She comes to visit to make herself feel better. She don't care nothin' about me."

I knew that he really did not mean that, but if I pushed the point it would just start a new fight. Gang members and their relationships with their mothers is very dangerous turf. Rather than pushing the point, I chose to change the subject. "Didn't you have a teacher or two who cared?"

"A teacher? Man, what type of sell out do you take me for?! Hell, I'd sooner trust a white like you, than trust one of them self-important liars."

"Why do you have such distrust for teachers?"

"Man, why do you want to know about my life? Is yours that boring and white or something?"

Rather than letting him know that his words bothered me, I just side-stepped them. "Let's just say I am curious. And besides, if you are busy telling me about life on the street, then I'm not yelling at you for putting your feet on the furniture or using swear words." Curtis slowly moved his feet from the chair to the floor and even moved to straighten up his back.

"Man, some teachers may know what they read about in books, but they don't know one thing about what it is like out on the streets. They don't even know about half the stuff they are trying to teach you about."

"What do you mean by that?" I asked Curtis, while trying to control any emotion in my voice.

"Exactly that. They give you an assignment. You try to follow it and what do they do? They make marks all over it. They mark you down, fail you and then embarrass you in front of everyone."

I was starting to get tired of Curtis's broken record of blaming racism for his own failures, but rather than expressing my own views now, I thought I would let Curtis get his full story out. "Give me an example."

"Man, I had this teacher for third grade. She gave us crayons and paper and told us to draw repeating patterns. I did what she told us. I drew changing colors in a 'repeating pattern,'" he said with a tone of total sarcasm. "She gave me an 'F'. When I got the paperback I got upset and went to tell her off. I showed it to her and showed her my pattern. It showed more work than anything the white kids had drawn to get an 'A'. When she finally understood what I had done, she gave me a 'C'.

"A 'C,' man! Other kids who had just drawn little birds all over the page or little shapes all over, they got 'A's. I drew a pattern so good that you had to really look to see it, and for this I got a fucking 'C'. Not only that, but she would not let me put it up on the board like the white kids did. That would mean she would have to admit to making a mistake. No white teacher would ever do that to me and this woman had it out for me from day one. If I said anything without raising my hand, I'd get sent to the office. The white kids just got warnings." Curtis's voice showed the timbre of his frustration. "They all treated me the same. When I left one teacher, she would tell my new teacher I was a troublemaker and that was it. If I stepped one inch out of line, I was in the principal's office for being a troublemaker. They did not want to deal with me themselves; they always sent me to the principal. The principal was never there when it happened. He never saw what happened, but he listened to what the teacher would say, and my words were ignored."

Curtis stopped talking and again turned to stare out the window at the trees. This was not an act. This was real anger. The anger of a nine-year-old betrayed by an adult he had been ordered to trust. Not that the teacher knew what she was doing. She might have done it by her ignorance and maybe even a little subconscious racism. I could not excuse what she had done, or explain it to this kid, but I now have to deal with what she had helped to create.

I heard enough to help me have sympathy for this youth who an hour earlier was threatening to kill me with his own hands. However, there was little I could do to help solve those past problems. I could not ask him to trust me. He believed that every adult who has ever asked him to trust them had lied to him and hurt him. I realized that if he was going to work with me, it would have to be his decision alone; I was not going to push it. Besides, it was not my responsibility to make him trust me. I first needed to make sure that he obeyed our rules and regulations. If I was actually able to get him to change his day-to-day behaviors while he was here, that was just a fringe benefit. I wanted to be able to help these kids, but my first priority was to get these kids to follow the house rules and keep us all safe. If I could not get them to do even that, then I would be the one getting in trouble. Besides, the only way we might ever know if we helped a kid was if we never saw them again in detention. This might mean that they had found alternatives to getting in trouble; unfortunately, it could also mean that the kid was killed.

It is a difficult line to walk, especially when you are sitting in a residence room and you feel like you are making progress. You hope that what you are doing will reach this kid. But as you sit in a chair next to him, you know deep in your heart, the kid's most likely trying to con you into believing that they want to change. You know they do this because they believe that if you trust them, they will be able to get away with more misbehavior. The closer you let yourself get to these kids, the better the chance they have to con you. It's times like this I have to remember the lottery tickets in my back pocket or my other dreams for my future.

Additional Information

Violent Confrontations

One of the worst events that can happen to anyone working with troubled kids is a violent confrontation. Not only are you risking your personal safety, but you need to consider how your actions will be "second-guessed" by others. Therefore, the last thing a youth worker ever wants to do is hit a kid, even in self-defense. If you do find yourself in a physical confrontation, you want to use the least amount of force to *REMOVE YOURSELF FROM THE SITUATION.* This means you will want to receive some proper training in self-defense and violence evasion. *DO NOT FIGHT BACK WHEN A STRONG PINCH TO THE ARMS WILL GIVE YOU AN ESCAPE FROM THE SITUATION.* Which would you rather explain to a police officer: "I only punched the kid unconscious after he tried to strangle me!" or "He tried to strangle me, so I pinched his arms and called you for assistance."

This is NOT a book about using violence, but rather avoiding it. Almost all violent situations start with a number of warning signs. By controlling your own emotions and responses to a kid, client, or student, you can better control situations, and possibly avoid violence. Before you can learn to control the reactions of others, you must learn to control your own.

When you find yourself in a difficult situation, the easiest thing to control is your breathing rate. Remind yourself to take long deep breaths; don't hyperventilate. Your body is pumping adrenaline into your bloodstream to heighten your awareness. This is good, because it helps you notice more of the events occurring around you, but it also limits your ability to think clearly and see other options for resolving the situation. The best way to combat this limitation is to be aware of how you are feeling and take your time before reacting to the situation. With the adrenaline in your bloodstream, your pulse will also increase. Unless you have spent years practicing controlling your pulse rate, the best way you will be able to get your pulse back down to a normal rate is to control your breathing. This is an important skill to practice before you need it.

Escalation vs. De-escalation

When working with others who use confrontation to get what they want, you need to be aware of the tools they may use to make you uncomfortable and gain control of the situation. The first indicator that someone might be looking for confrontation is their distance from you. Each of us has a space around us. We are uncomfortable if someone we do not know and trust enters this space. The amount of this space varies from person to person and culture to culture. One way that high-risk youths might try to make you uncomfortable is by entering your personal space during a face-to-face confrontation. They may also wave their arms into your safety zone in an attempt to make you feel that you must defend yourself. Their goal is to make you feel uncomfortable, violated, or that you need to defend yourself. Remember, if you make physical contact with them first, they will argue that anything they did was in self-defense.

To deal with "space invaders" you need to be aware of what they are doing. During confrontations which have the potential of becoming dangerous, slowly move away from the aggressor, while using body language to hold your ground. Remember to keep your eyes focused on the face of the agitator, your shoulders back, and your hands in front of you. Do not let them make you feel uncomfortable, but at the same time do not let them force you to retreat into a corner.

Another method some might find useful is actually to close the distance between yourself and the aggressor. This is escalating the confrontation. Be careful, as this can bring the confrontation to the next level, or it may make the youth back off. The method you use will depend on the situation, the risk of actual physical harm, your physical presence and awareness, and how well you deal with confrontation. This method should only be used when you want to convince the youth that you can be more dangerously aggressive than them, and they really do not want to attack you. The problem with this approach is that you may be required to back up your words with actions, which can cause you difficulties.

Another method a client uses to control a situation is by voice. Yelling and different tones in a voice can increase the stress level of a confrontation. Be aware of your situation. Remember not only to listen to the youth with whom you are working, but also be aware of your own reactions to what the youth is doing. Listen to yourself. Is your voice getting higher pitched? Are you yelling also? How quickly are you speaking? Take control of yourself and the situation. De-escalate by keeping your voice and volume in a standard range. Try to speak slowly and carefully. Remember that every word you speak will be used against you, so be careful what you say.

A final escalation tool that will be used against you is body language: both theirs and yours. A youth will raise his hands over his head, and move them in threatening gestures. The top of his body will move forward of his legs and feet. The muscles in the face will tighten. How will you react? If you are escalating, then tighten your muscles, but be careful what you do with your arms. You will want to be ready to defend yourself, but you do not want to encourage your client to actually physically attack or harm you. You could be blamed for starting the fight you were hired to keep from starting.

If you choose to de-escalate by moving away from the youth, you still need to be careful. The youth could still attack and you will need to be ready to protect yourself, so be aware of where your arms are resting. Keep your arms and hands in front of you, either by your side or across your chest. Do not interlock your arms, as they need to be able to move quickly to use your arms to protect you. Try to keep your posture non-threatening, but with your feet spread a little apart for balance. Finally, control your facial muscles. Some counselors might try to smile off the confrontation. In other words, "I see what you are trying to do, but I am not going to play this game. I am smiling at you because I am in control of the situation."

Escalation and de-escalation is just one area where each situation and the type of person you are will affect how you handle the situation. You will use different methods in a confrontation with a four-foot-ten-inch eleven-year-old than you might use in a confrontation with a six-foot fifteen-year-old. Also remember that the type of program you are in will also dictate the approaches you can use. A boot camp model will require you to be more confrontational and direct than a less restrictive model.

Trust!!!

When you start working in any new environment or with any new youth, you will learn how important the illusion of trust is to your relationship with your clients. Most clients feel that they have been lied to by every adult they know. They do not know who you are and how you will react to different situations. Be prepared for a "baptism of fire" when you start, as the youths, together or individually, will try to test you to see how you react to stressful situations. One of my experiences working in a group home started when my coworker went outside for a smoke break. The youths started a food fight to see how much would be tolerated and how I would try to regain control of the situation. I later learned that my coworker was in on the plan. He wanted to see how I would react or if I would give up and quit. Much to everyone's surprise, myself included, I managed to take control by sending selected youths to their rooms. While my coworker supervised these selected individuals, the remaining kids cleaned up the mess with my assistance. The longer I worked at the center, the fewer tests of my authority occurred. New incoming youths already heard about me from other past clients and knew how I would deal with them. In short, it took about three weeks of tests before the youths learned I could be trusted to be fair, but that I had certain expectations of them and their behaviors. You will not earn their trust with your words, but only with the actions they observe in you. However, remember that all of this trust is just an illusion, as the clients are still trying to learn ways to cause mischief and get away with various rule violations.

This is another place where you need to be aware of yourself and your reactions to different situations. It could be very easy to assume that each of these youths were equally responsible for the food fight. However, nobody likes it when others make negative assumptions about them and their behavior. Part of the test that these youths put me through was to find out if I could learn who was actually responsible and act accordingly. In my program, I was required that if the group misbehaved, the group should be held accountable. To get around this, I used the kids whom I had not sent to their rooms to help clean up the mess. So they too were punished for letting the food fight occur.

As a youth worker you will also be required to work within and between the policies of your employer, your own beliefs, and appropriate responses. It will be up to you to find ways of dealing with situations with which you are comfortable. You must comply with your employer's expectations to avoid termination and to protect yourself from legal responsibility should anything happen while you are at work. However, these youths can tell when you are not comfortable taking certain actions and they will use it against you if you let them.

MAJOR POINTS

1)   Know yourself!!! Know which methods will work for you and which will not! Know what you are comfortable doing and what you will not do under any situation.
2)   Learn how to de-escalate a confrontational situation. Learn methods that are comfortable for you, and keep looking for new methods.
3)   Understand that as you do not like others to make assumptions about you, others don't like it either. Start learning your own biases so you can be aware of them. They can be made to work against you.

CLASS ACTIVITIES

1)   Divide the class into groups of three. Two of the group members will have a heated argument. The topics of the disagreement should be directly relevant to the students involved. It is the responsibility of the third member to end the confrontation. It is the responsibility of the instructor or other observers to encourage the confrontation. Each person should have to take a turn as peacemaker. After the exercise the small groups will discuss how each person

felt about being a participant in the confrontation. How did each person do when working as the peacemaker? Were they able to work with methods of de-escalation which were appropriate for them? Could the person use or overcome their size, strength or gender differences when they were in the peacemaker role? What could they have done better? Repeat exercise as needed.

2) Form students into groups of two. The first person's goal is to start an argument with person number two. Person number two's goal is to try to keep control of the situation. Work at these roles for five minutes and switch roles. Class discussion: What is the person who is trying to start the fight doing? What is the person who is trying to avoid the argument doing? What works or does not work in avoiding a fight? How did you feel when you were confronted? Did this affect how you responded? How did you feel when you were confronting the other person? How might this affect the actions you might take when dealing with high-risk youths?

3) Break into teams of two people. Each person takes five minutes to describe a third person to their partner. After hearing the description the listener will write down what they have learned about the person who has been described to them (two pages minimum). Switch papers. Is this paper about the person you described? What have they assumed about the person you described? Were these assumptions accurate? How do you think the person you have described might feel about this written description of them? Would they feel complimented or insulted?

Chapter 2
The Home Front

QUESTIONS TO THINK ABOUT AS YOU READ

1) How do you feel at the end of the work or school day?

2) How will your family and friends feel about you working in a possibly dangerous situation?

3) How do you feel about working with state or agency Social Workers? Are those feelings based on personal experience, assumptions or academic training?

4) How do you feel when you are observing a conflict? Can these emotions help or hinder you during an intervention? Why and how?

5) What changes in your approach might be necessary to help you better deal with conflicts?

6) To what extent are you willing, or should the state go, to protect a child from abuse?

7) What if you are wrong about the abuse? When might you be doing more harm than good?

READING

It always seemed like an eternity before 1600 hours arrived. I'd sit and watch the clock until it was time to go home. However, when it was finally time to go, I did not want to leave. When everything seemed in order and my replacement had assured me at least four times, "Don't worry, I have the keys," I could finally leave. Jumping into my twelve-year-old, ¾-ton cargo van, I always felt like I was forgetting something. I would check my pockets one more time. Finding nothing that did not belong there, it was time to surrender the keys and try to get that engine to turn over just one more time to take me home. After my checks, I turned the key to hear the melodic roaring sound which meant that I had spilled enough oil over the engine case. . . this time.

It was always a long drive home. My father often accused me of flying low over the freeway. It was not that I was speeding, but in a vehicle as old and as large as mine, just approaching the legal limit was enough to make it seem like I was moving twice as fast as I really was. I had figured that no officer would have given this old battle wagon a speeding ticket. They would probably look at the speed on their radar gun, and decide it was time to take it in for re-calibration.

I finally reached my exit. I exited off of one freeway onto another. But this second throughway was usually a parking lot. I opted to get off at the first exit and take a side street and two minutes later I was home as usual. There was Beatrice, my newly wedded wife, waiting for me. Today was one of those special days when I could open the car door and there she was. "And to what do I owe this special privilege?" I asked.

"It's nice to have you home, sweetie. I've gotten a lot done and I can just relax for the rest of the evening. And how was your day, dear?"

"It was a good day at work, dear. I only received two death threats today," I said, watching her facial expression change from a pleasant greeting to a grimace. "But those we worked out," I continued as I slid out of the van, and grabbed my things.

She pulled me to her to give me a hug. "Dear, do me a favor."

"Yes?"

"Promise me you'll start looking for another job?"

"No."

She took a deep breath and slowly said, "Dear, I realize you feel you need to do this. However, it scares me the number of days you tell me that you have been threatened. I would just feel better if you could find another place to do your work. I know to you these are just empty threats, but one of these days they might mean something more. I am really concerned that someday you might find yourself in a hospital or worse."

"The kid was not going to hurt me. He just wanted to get my attention. We worked it out. And I might have even made some progress with him, but I am not going to hold my breath."

She lowered her arms from our embrace so I could close the car door. We went into the house. We still lived with her parents so that we could afford to live on my joke of a paycheck, and so I could pay off my student loans. Her father was pleased I was working, but nervous about the type of work I was doing. This came from a man who served 20 years in the military.

It was the start of my Monday evening shift, around 1600 hours, and I was just finishing reading the logs when the doorbell rang. I turned and asked my coworkers if we were expecting a visit from someone.

"Oh, yes. A social worker from the State Department of Family Services called and said she was coming to see Curtis Jones."

I went to the door and asked to see her identification. She showed me a state card with a picture that *actually* almost looked like her. I invited her in and had her sign the visitor's log. While explaining to her the visiting rules, I called Curtis into the small classroom we had in the facility and invited the social worker to join us.

Curtis turned to me and asked who this lady was; I looked at her to see if she would take the lead in the conversation. "Curtis, my name is Jane Stevens; I'm from the State Department of Family Services." She handed Curtis a card. He looked at it for a moment and put it in his pocket. His face showed that he could have cared less, and I knew that the next time I saw that card I would be pulling it out of the washing machine in wet, soggy pieces.

"I am here to talk with you at the request of the court and your mother."

"What you mean my mother!" Curtis suddenly got angry. His eyes changed in an instant from withdrawn glances to fired intensity. His posture changed from a slouched position in his chair to bolt upright, as if he might jump out of his chair at any moment.

I prepared myself to intervene in the developing conflict. "Calm down, man. Let the woman finish what she has to say."

Curtis looked at me. His eyes showed the fire of the emotions her comments had triggered. I just looked at Curtis and showed with a downward motion of my hand that I understood how he felt, but that I needed him to calm down. Slowly Curtis lowered his shoulders and lowered himself back into his chair.

She continued, "One of the Juvenile Court judges has asked me to speak with you and your mother to see if there might be a better housing situation than what you have here. We are concerned that with your mother working as hard as she currently is, that she might not be able to give you the type of supervision you need."

"Are you saying that my mother is not a good mother!? Are you saying that you know what I need better than my own mother!?" Curtis exploded and jumped out of his chair.

I realized that she had done it. Ms. Stevens had done the one thing guaranteed to make this meeting the most painful. Without meaning to, she had insulted Curtis's mother. Even I knew that insulting a gang kid's mother was a bad move. I had seen it numerous times when kids were complaining about their parents. If another kid, or even worse, a well-meaning young counselor, agrees with the complaining youth that his parents are unfair or abusive, the kid will suddenly turn on their supporter. A youth can insult or complain about his own mother, but if someone else questions a mother's abilities, the new questioner is in serious trouble. Without meaning to, Ms. Stevens had now violated this most important rule.

Now it was Ms. Stevens who was looking at me to take the lead. "Curtis, I don't know what she is trying to get at, but we should at least let her say what she has to. If you lose control of your temper, you might be making a big mistake."

"It's not me who is making a mistake insulting my mother!"

"I don't think Ms. Stevens meant to insult your mother. I think she was just trying to say that your mother is overworked." I looked to the social worker to do her job. After all, this was her interview and her investigation.

Ms. Stevens started again. "The judge wants me to find out if you might be better off in a home where the responsible adult's only job is to look after you and your interests, rather than doing that as well as working 8 to 12 hours a day."

"Why are you talking to me about it?" Curtis asked.

"What you want is a very important part of how these decisions will be made."

"Don't lie to me! What I want has nothing to do with what you are going to do. You know what you are going to do with me long before you came here. Every time one of you social workers comes to see me, you always say that what I want is important; but every time I tell you what I want, you never give it to me."

Ms. Stevens asked naively, "What is it you want?"

"I want you and your kind to leave me and my family alone. Every time I tell you people that, you tell me whatever recommendation you are going to make and you read it off a form that you typed up before you even came here."

"Well, Mr. Jones, here is the form on which I will put my recommendations, and you can see that it is blank." The frustration and a bit of anger in her voice was coming to the surface.

"How do I know you don't have another one in your folder or back at your office?" Curtis asked in his sharpest tone.

I realized it was not my place to make this meeting work, but I thought I might be able to help. "Ms. Stevens, will you please step outside for a bit; you might want to find a comfortable chair. Please close the door on your way out."

As soon as the door was closed, Curtis started in on the social worker. "Where does she get off coming in here and telling me about what's good for me and my family? What right does she have telling me what is good for me? How can she say that my mother ain't fit?"

I realized that Curtis was not really listening to what she was saying. He was not really ignoring her, but rather reading more into what she was saying than might have been there. He was not just testing her responses. It was clear that there was more to Curtis's anger than just missing this afternoon's reruns and talking to this particular social worker.

"Curtis," I interrupted, "I don't want you to feel like I'm prying into your life again, but I get this feeling that it is not just this social worker that is getting under your skin."

"Man, you can't trust any of those fucking social workers. They are either lazy and want to get you off their desk or they are stupid and don't have a clue about what life is really like on the streets," Curtis said, as he flung himself about the room.

"Curtis, would you like to calm down and explain to me why you have such an intense hatred of social workers?"

"Man, why should you care?"

"Who says I do? It will just make my job and your life a bit easier to tell me a story that might just be true." However, whether it was true or not, Curtis started to calm down and sit down. But the fire had not yet left his eyes.

"Man, I have not trusted those people since I met my first one when I was eight. She come into the house without even being asked in. I told her that my mother was at work and would not be home for an hour. She just took herself a seat in my house and made it look like she owned the place. I did not ask her to come in and sit down in my kitchen. I tried to ignore her and I continued to look after my kid brother."

"You're saying she was rude?" I asked in what I knew was a leading question.

"Rude? You ain't heard nothin' yet. When my mother finally did get home, she got rude. This lady asked my mother what kind of parent would leave an eight-year-old and a five-year-old home alone together. My mother tried to explain to this lady about why she worked. My mother asked that bitch if she wanted my mother to quit her job, look after us and live on welfare. This just made the social worker more rude."

"More rude?" I asked. I did not really care that he was swearing. I was more interested in letting him vent his anger, calm down, and finish the interview so we could get rid of the social worker who was waiting on the other side of the door.

"This woman that had no right to even be in our house. And here she was threatenin' to take me and my brother with her. My mother tried to explain that she had the neighbors come to look in on my bro and me. This did not satisfy this bitch. Finally, my mother told this lady what she wanted to make her go away. The 'ho' finally agreed to leave if my mother would try to work fewer hours, sign up for some welfare and take some parenting classes. My mother was angry for a week. And who had to deal with her? Not some snooty lady from the state. Oh no, I had to be with her and now she was really angry. To make a mother that angry and then to leave her with us, that was real child abuse. That week was worse than any beating my mother had ever given me.

"When my mother finally got around to doing what that bitch wanted, it was crazy. She almost lost her job, but got out of five hours of work a week. She then spent five hours down at the welfare office per week to get help and went to those stupid classes two times a week at night. On those nights I was left not only to look after Luther during the afternoon, but I also had to cook dinner and put my brother to bed. Every night she would have less time to spend to be with Luther and me. On the nights she had those stupid classes, she would come home even later and more tired after we had already gone to bed. She would complain about what a waste of time it all was. The 'parenting' teacher did not have a clue about what our lives were like. So after that bitch order my mother spend more time with us, but we never saw her!"

"The social worker or your mother?" I asked.

"My mother was so busy doin' what that bitch wanted, she had no time to spend with me or my bro."

I wanted to get Curtis calmed down so that Ms. Stevens could do her interview, but it was clear that Curtis had a little more that he wanted to get off his chest, so I let him continue.

"I thought that social worker was the rudest person around. I thought wrong. After putting up with her and her shit for two months, my mother got told that she was being assigned a new social worker. When my mother asked why, she was told that it was standard fuckin' procedure."

I gave Curtis a glare with my right eye, to remind him about his language. He had to look at me a second to remember that he needed to calm down and be careful how he spoke.

"The new social worker came into our home and started questioning everything that my mother was doing. She wanted to know why my mother was getting welfare when she should be working. When my mother tried to explain to this bitch why she was getting welfare this lady just went off. She told my mother to either get another job or work more hours at her current job. My mother told her that she would be more than happy to.

"Suddenly this woman who had no right to be yelling at my mother in her own house stopped and looked at my mother, like, real funny. She asked my mother if she would rather work than get welfare. My mother told her yes. Suddenly the lady changed, she became nice, but only for the rest of the evening.

"A few days later we got this letter. It said that my mother had gotten the money by lying. No one accuses my mother of lying. It also said my mother had to give back all of the money she had received. She then had to miss another day of work to spend another day at the welfare office and explain what had happened. When she came home, she told me that she had lost a day's pay and all that she got was a stupid promise to 'look into it'.

"Two weeks later we got a letter telling us to ignore the first letter. No apology, no admitting my mother was not a liar, no nothing.

"Was this the end of it?! Hell no!" Curtis was again trying to get out of his chair. I motioned for him to remain seated with my hand. "For the next three or four years the school kept calling us in, because I would not go to school. And when I did go to school, I kept getting in trouble. They would call my mother and tell her that if she did not miss more work to come and talk to them, they would call the state again. This would mean having to deal with another damned social worker. I don't know what the school had against my momma, but I sure don't trust them after all the trash they talked against my momma.

"It was them who called the state the first time and put us through that. And then they kept threatenin' to do it to us again if my mother did not do what they wanted. My momma keeps telling me not to worry, because she knows what they trying to do. Momma told me that all the school want was to make us move so that they won't have to deal with me or my bro no more. My momma ain't no fool. She knows that the school don't like me or my bro, but she'll be damned if she'll let a bunch of *white know everything, do nothing 'social workers'* force her to do anything."

I finally interrupted his tirade. "I know you have a lot of reasons not to trust social workers, but not all of them are evil, lazy or stupid. Ms. Stevens seems intelligent and she does not look like a demon to me. Besides, the only way that we are going to get rid of her is to answer her questions so she can leave."

"She actually looks sort of friendly," Curtis started, "but that doesn't mean that I trust her or that I'll say anything against my mother to her. I'll do this just so she'll leave, but that don't mean I'm go'n to tell her anything she wants to hear," Curtis concluded.

"I don't expect you to trust her, but I do need you to either work with her or just look like you are answering her questions. Can you do that so we can get this over with, rid of her, and get on with our lives?"

"Yeah, I'll try."

"Thanks man," I said as I got up to let the social worker back into the room.

I wanted to start the meeting over and tried to set the tone. "I have explained to Curtis that he does not have to trust you to work with you. Curtis has also explained to me why he has problems dealing with people from your agency; however, Curtis has agreed to work through this with you."

Ms. Stevens decided to take my lead. "Curtis, I realize that you probably had bad experiences dealing with people from my office. To be honest, many people have. First I want to apologize to you for that. Can you accept my apology?"

"Yeah, sure," Curtis said, in a tone showing less than complete attention.

"Second, let me explain to you what is going on. Because of your numerous problems with the law, the court has ordered me to meet with you, your mother, and your probation officer. You are the first I have met with. No one, except the judge, has asked me to do anything. The judge has asked me to find out if you would be better off in a group home. I do not like group homes and from the sound of it, neither do you. If you are willing to give me some help, we might be able to convince the judge to let you stay with your mother."

Curtis looked like he was only mildly paying attention to what Ms. Stevens had to say. He knew that she was telling him at least a partial truth. He still did not really trust her or even care to listen to her. Besides, his mind appeared more focused on the clean chalkboard on the wall and how he could leave his graffiti tag all over it.

Jane, however, continued undaunted. "I have a set of questions I need to ask you. If after I am finished, there is something you want to add, I will be glad to stay here and listen until you are done. I will put all of your comments into my report. Is this a problem?"

"No, let's just get this over with."

The rest of the interview actually went fairly well. Ms. Stevens would ask questions and Curtis would answer them with as few words as he could. When Jane was finished, Curtis tried to be very clear that he did not want the state to interfere with him and his mother. Jane told Curtis that if his mother agreed with his opinions, then odds were that the state would also want to leave him and his mother alone. However, it was the judge who they were going to have to convince. I don't know if Curtis actually believed her, but he was not going to argue with her. Forty-five minutes after it had restarted, the interview was over. I could feel myself relax as the door closed behind the social worker. However, this was short-lived.

The next thing I heard was my boss calling me into her office. The hair on the back of my neck started to stand on end, as I walked down the hallway to her office. Thoughts of what I could have done wrong went racing through my head. Had the social worker complained to her about being left out in the hallway for so long?

When I finally got into her office, all she wanted to know was if I could work a double shift tomorrow. I was so relieved that I was not in trouble again that I said "yes" without thinking. It was an hour later before I realized that I had just volunteered to work the two shifts from Hell, back to back.

ADDITIONAL INFORMATION

Friends, Family and Work

When you get your first job you will have a mix of emotions. While you will be happy that a major worry has been dealt with, you will also have many concerns. What will your supervisor really be like? How will you and your coworkers interact? Did you make the correct career choice? These are questions that only you can answer. There are some other questions you may want to think about.

Depending on your age and progress on your personal life path, you will have different life concerns. Stop and think for a moment. Who do you call family? Are they your parents, a wife, a fiancé or a group of close friends? Stop for a moment and think about all of the people who surround you and care about you. Now, with all of these people in mind, think of how they will react to your working with high-risk youths? You may feel you do not need to worry when you hear a threat from a client. However, will the people who care about you feel the same way?

In the start of chapter two I wrote about an actual homecoming. This was a real event, not fiction. My father-in-law served in the military for twenty years. He hung around friends who loved to tell "war stories" about times they had taken stupid risks. After two weeks on the job at juvenile detention, he would try to leave the room to avoid hearing about a rough day at work. He was supportive of what I was doing, but he also was worried about me. What if I misjudged a threat and a youth tried to act one out? You will need to think about how your work will affect your family and friends. How they interact with you will affect how well you will be able to perform on the job.

You will also need to think about how the stress of your job will affect you. Remember, you need to take time to do things for yourself. Since your days off will be different from your friends', you will need to work harder to make sure you spend time with them. Take time to work on your hobbies and home projects. If you have issues from your own childhood or past, take the time to get professional help to work these out. Do these things, not only to reduce your own stress, but also to reduce those tools the youths can use against you on the job.

Salary Reality

The actual income you can expect to receive will vary depending on your career choice, geographic location and type of agency for which you are working. Entry level jobs are notorious for not paying a lot. Therefore, you will need to take some steps to make your pay go further.

Try to save money on transportation costs. If you cannot find a job in walking distance from where you are living, try to be within one bus route. If that does not work, remember that while a newer car may save you money on gas and unscheduled maintenance, compare these costs to that of a used vehicle. Ironically, an old reliable gas guzzler is still cheaper than a newer car with payments.

Learn to avoid unnecessary expenses such as eating at restaurants too often. It is cheapest to eat a prepared meal from home. It can cost four times more to buy a pre-prepared meal at a convenience store. Eating at restaurants can cost you four to eight times as much as a home meal. By planning your eating and appetite you can control these expenses. Planning like this can save you money in many areas of your budget.

It is tempting to spend money the moment you get it; this is a trap. Remember that you have education debts to pay off, and you must start saving money early. You do not know what unexpected expenses are just around the corner. You can either be prepared for these expenses, or they can bury you in debt.

It is most important that you take the time now to learn and develop good spending and savings habits. Do not plan on having more money tomorrow to cover today's debts. Only spend money that you actually have. When you do spend money, make sure you are doing it as an investment in your future. Examples of this behavior include getting your car fixed before it breaks, buying good work clothes, and putting money into your retirement account. Finally, do not live on credit card debt. These cards are designed to make their investors rich off of those who use them. They are set up so you will be paying interest on restaurant lunch for years to come.

Identification

It should be noted that none of the staff members ever use their last name in front of the clients. This is done for personal protection. With just your full name and a little personal information, a criminal can find out where you live, what car you drive, or even take your identity to use your credit. With just a name and a city, someone can find a phone number and address in a phone book or on-line. While many youth workers take the risks of their career choice in stride, it is not appropriate for one to put their family at risk.

Realities of social work

No matter what field of youth work you are in, if you are there long enough you will come in contact with a state social worker. This is not a book about social work, but as a youth worker you will need to know something about what they do and how they do it. There are two major approaches which child safety social workers might use in their approach; each has benefits and weaknesses. These are summarized below, so that you will know what approach is being used.

The older method is a child-centered practice. This practice calls on the social worker to protect the child first and the family second. These social workers are more likely to take a child out of a bad situation sooner. This may not be in the best interests of the family as a whole, but it removes the child from possible dangerous situations sooner. These social workers who are more likely to remove a child when there may be less legal cause than the public thinks is appropriate.

The family-centered model tries to look at the child in the context of the family. This requires the social worker to try to offer services to the family and to take only gradual steps as needed. These social workers will try to keep the family together in a functional unit as long as the social worker thinks they safely can. This sometimes means that a child will be left in a potentially dangerous situation. If the child is removed, they may be placed with a different adult relative or in foster care. Limited community resources for assisting families can also weaken this approach to social work.

Both approaches have their strengths and weaknesses. Also, many states officially declare the use of a family-centered practice, while their social workers are actually pressured to use a child-centered approach for liability reasons. In short, learn about the social workers and be familiar with the practices of your own state.

There are also many types of social workers. In one office, the social workers were broken down into three separate teams. The first person a family might have had contact with was the investigator. Their job was to investigate serious allegations of child abuse and neglect. They interviewed the child and family to learn if there were serious problems and what services might be appropriate to help the family or child. This can mean anything from closing the case, to in-home services, to removing the child into state care while a parent or child receives special services.

If a child is removed, or a case looks like it will take longer than the time set by state policy, the case could be handed over to a long-term unit. Again, this varies depending on the size and divisions within the individual field office. In some offices there are two long-term units. One works with youth below ten and the other works with youth over ten. Each local office may be organized differently, depending on the number of personnel and cases handled. These variations can have an unfortunate effect on the target families.

The first time the parents of a target family learn about an investigation is usually when they receive a phone call from a state social worker informing them that an allegation has been made and that their school-age children have already been interviewed. Many parents feel that they have already been convicted when they hear this. They do not know what is going on, or what their children might have told this total stranger from the state. The family finally meets the social worker only after the first interviews with the child(ren) are completed. In some states, the family has the right to refuse to cooperate with the investigation. Unless the social worker already has gathered enough evidence to prove to a judge that a child is at serious risk of abuse or neglect, this refusal to assist means the social worker may have to close the case. If the family agrees to cooperate, as most do, then the social worker usually either informs them that the allegation was unfounded (as over 60% are), or that while there are issues of concern, these are minor and most families can address them on their own. From personal experience, five percent of the cases investigated had problems serious enough to keep a case open for continued work. In only two percent of the cases did the state actually remove the child and provide services to the family and children separately. (Please note: these statistics are based on my personal experience, the numbers provided during state training and information from other social workers. Since child abuse files are sealed from public access, it is almost impossible for an independent study to be conducted and accurate statistics to be compiled.)

In the last two examples of state agencies, the case would then be handed off to the long-term units. The younger children would be assigned to one long-term team and the older children to the other. What this means to the contact family is that as soon as they have met one social worker and learned what the social worker expects, the case is then handed over to another social worker who may have completely different expectations. Many families come to resent the state not only for intervening in their family, but also for the changing expectations placed on them.

In response to this, many families will tell state social workers almost anything to get the officials to go away. Family members listen to the way questions are asked and give answers they think the social worker will want to hear. Good social workers will learn to look at the surroundings of the house and how the parents interact with the children during any visit. Some parents say how much they love their children, while yelling at their child to leave them alone as they are talking to the social worker. This can be one indicator of serious problems.

Social workers have a difficult job to do, and a reputation which can get in the way of doing that job. If you come in contact with a social worker, listen to them carefully and try to learn what they are interested in. If you ever become a social worker, remember that your presence, your approach, and the way you conduct yourself will be affecting everything you see and hear.

MAJOR POINTS

1) There is an interrelationship between your work and your family life. Be prepared to deal with family and friends who are uncomfortable with how you make a living.

2) Social workers are doing a difficult job. They are responsible for protecting children, while working within legal limitations and their office's structure.

3) In your professional career you will come in contact with a number of different professionals. Do not let your personal biases affect how you deal with them. Each person is different and may approach their job in a manner you might find different from what you expect or choose for yourself, if it was your job.

CLASS ACTIVITIES

1) Split the class into pairs. Have teams brainstorm a list of people who are important in their lives. Narrow the list down to the top five for each student. Have each student write a paragraph per person on their list about how that person might react to the student's taking a high-risk job.

2) Using a random method, divide the class into pairs. One student will be the investigator, and the other the accused. The professor will assign the number and ages of the children in question to each pair of students. The investigator is to create and write down an allegation of either child abuse or neglect against the accused student. The investigator shall question the accused student not only about the accusation, but also about their methods of discipline, feeding, parental interaction with children, clothing, housing and schooling.

The professor will hand out to each investigator a small paper bag containing a card. On the card the professor will list six items commonly found in a student's backpack. These may include, but are not limited to, books, ruler, pens, paper, medication, diabetic kit, soda can, cigarettes, matches, roll your own papers and a bag of tobacco, etc. The student being investigated need not be told the specific items in their backpack, until questioned about them. The investigator will open the bag and inquire as to how each item is used and the possible threat they might pose to their "children."

REMEMBER: this is to be a LEGAL INVESTIGATION. Should the accused student refuse access to the investigator, the investigator SHALL respect that refusal, but may try to convince the subject to assist with their investigation. Do not break any federal, state or local laws in conducting this investigation. If you have any questions, check with your professor.

The investigator will write a four-page paper on the results of their investigation. This paper should not only cover the original accusation, but also any concern that the investigator might have developed during the investigation.

The accused will write a two-page paper on what they felt like during all parts of the investigation. They should also write about what they would do the same or differently if they were the investigator.

The students will share their papers with each other and discuss the results. Did the accused student agree with the conclusions of the investigator? Were the investigators conclusions influenced by their background or culture?

Now do this exercise again, but switch roles. The new investigator should keep in mind how they felt when they were the accused, during their investigation. Have a classroom discussion after both students have completed both papers. What have the students learned about investigations and child abuse? How can investigators do their jobs without violating the rights of the parents? How much investigating is abuse of the rights of the investigated? What is the appropriate boundary between protecting children and protecting innocent families?

Chapter 3
An Education in Educating High-Risk Youths

QUESTIONS TO THINK ABOUT AS YOU READ

1) What were your educational experiences like? How do you explain your own educational successes and failures? How would this affect your outlook toward going to school?

2) Who were your favorite teachers? What qualities did they share? Were they always kind? How demanding were they?

READING

The next morning, I arrived at work at 0650 hours. We used military time, not because we followed anything close to strict military protocol, but to keep the boss from getting confused between a.m. and p.m. As usual, I was early for my shift. I preferred to show up early, as I could never depend on traffic being light. My coworkers were glad to see me and were used to leaving the minute I arrived, regardless of the actual time. For the one I was working with, it gave them someone new to complain to about the person who just left. It was our standard morning ritual.

I entered the front door with my usual sarcastic line. "Hello, I represent the legal firm of Dewey, Cheatem and Howe . . .," not that my coworkers actually paid any attention. My morning readings were waiting for me. First I read the resident's board to see who was new, who had room restriction, who was due to be released and who had to be reminded five times to take their medication. I then read the main log to find out what had occurred on the two shifts prior to my own. If I was particularly energetic, I would then read all of the new kids' files to try to learn their convictions and any background information I could find. I still had about a half an hour before I would go wake up my young charges.

Morning wake-up was sort of a sadistic pleasure for me. I had already been up for two hours and each knock on the door and "Good morning" was greeted with either a mumble or a, "Man Josh, why can't you just let us sleep in?" On rare occasions, I would come to a room where the resident was already awake and ready to go, with a clean room. These youths earned themselves a head shake of approval or a verbal, "Nice room." After half an hour of prodding, everyone was up and ready for breakfast.

I volunteered Timothy, a kid who was in the program for over a week, to help me set up breakfast. Our food came prepared for us by another facility owned by our company. They delivered it ready to serve in large metal trays. I would actually serve the food, but Tim would set and carry the full plates to the tables. Ten minutes later, breakfast was on the table.

While breakfast was being eaten, I posted the morning chores list onto the kitchen wall. As part of our program, each resident is given a particular responsibility for the upkeep of the house. The chore lists are always greeted with whining, complaining and, "Man, why do I have to vacuum? I'm not paid to be here." I found out, or was taught by more senior staff, that it is easier to post the list and get out of the way. If you just let them do the chores, the kids will finish their tasks quicker than if you ride the clients about chores. These kids have a problem with authority standing over their shoulders, forcing them to do anything. By letting the youths do their chores on their own, I was able to avoid the passive resistance that direct micromanagement would have created. Besides, if they have no one to resist against, they might as well get their chores done so they can watch TV.

Finally when the chores are completed, I turned on the TV. Usually at least one of the new kids refuses to do their chores until all of the kids explain to him no chores, no TV. This level of peer pressure usually got the tasks completed quickly. With the youths being babysat by the TV, I had fifteen minutes to catch up on paperwork, update the logs, give out medication and get ready to take the youths to school. Just when I thought I was on top of things, the doorbell rang and it was time for my coworker to go home. This meant catching the newcomer up on the events of the day and finding out how it would affect both of our days.

Finally the magic time arrived. I got up and turned off the morning cartoons. "Gentlemen, go upstairs and use the restroom, get your coats, and get ready for school." I carefully ignored the chorus of complaints. Slowly the people moved toward the stairs to go up to their rooms.

Over the next five minutes my charges were slowly herded together into the foyer. Each kid was both dreading and looking forward to going to school. They felt they could do without the long boring classes, but I knew that deep down they looked forward to seeing their friends and catching up on the news from the streets. However, since the place we were going was called school, these youths felt it was their obligation to loudly protest this required intrusion in their lives.

Whenever we left the building, I always felt like the biblical shepherd leading his flock. My coworker stayed back at the office and helped the supervisor with the paperwork of running a program. So I was responsible to supervise all of the youths. I always let my seven to twelve kids go out the door first. I then followed behind. There were two reasons why I did this; first, it gave me more control. Second, I never let these kids walk behind me because then I could not see what they were doing. It was a short walk around the building to our van. Once I unlocked the door, the squabbles began over who got to sit where. To me it seemed rather silly, as the school was only two blocks away and all of the seats were equally uncomfortable. But to the kids, getting the seat they wanted showed where they were in the "pecking order." The top kids would never agree to sit in a middle seat with no windows.

I instructed my charges to put on their seatbelts for our short trip. However, there was no way for me to actually watch all twelve seatbelts and the road around me. When we arrived at the school, the kids jumped out and tried to get in past the metal detector before I caught them. I just called them all back to the metal detector to make sure enough it did not go off. It's not that I really worried about it, but these kids wanted to feel that they were somehow getting around the rules. It was part of my job to teach these kids to follow these rules. So every day they tried to sneak around the metal detector, and every day I just called them back to go through it.

We then moved to the cafeteria where the other students were waiting. My youths sat in the back of the room, in chairs set aside for us. They quickly looked around to find their friends around the room and started to catch up on the news from the street by shouting at each other across the room. They found out who got burned for what, who was back on the streets, and who was injured or killed last night or over the weekend. At times I tried to discourage this type of talk, but usually I just let it go. This was the school's program and the principal got offended if I took corrective action against any youth who was not in my program. I took advantage of the time to talk with the teachers. They wanted to know how many kids I had with me, if I had any kids that needed close supervision, or if anything had happened to any of the kids they have worked with for a long time.

The principal finally walked into the room. She was a short woman with broad shoulders in a gray power suit which was buttoned up in the front and two sizes too small. She carried her air of self-importance about her, and everyone in the room knew not to push their luck with her, no matter how tempting it might be. She surveyed around the entire room, as if to say that she was the queen of all she could see, and she was not happy about the view. Suddenly she moved her head in an expression of extreme disapproval.

"Mr. Ortega, stand up." A youth slowly rose from his chair. "Why can I see your underwear, young man?" Before the youth could even utter a sound, "Pull them pants up . . . you know better than to come here dressed like that."

The youth pulled on his pants. They came up to his waist, then fell a few inches back. With a nod of self-approval, the principal gestured to him to sit down. He glided back down into his chair and slouched even further than he was before, as if hoping the table would hide him from the principal's glare. She then continued to survey her realm.

After what seemed like an eternity, she finally began the litany of the daily schedule. When she was done with her speech, she finally let the other teachers speak. My kids sat in their chairs with a mixture of staring into space and tedious boredom. I was always impressed by the fact that the kids actually sat still through this morning ritual without starting a riot. When the speeches concluded, we were slowly dismissed to our class one group at a time.

The first class was English and it could actually be fun. The teacher had learned how to get the students to do what she wanted without realizing that they were actually learning something. She encouraged the students to write about their experiences from the streets. The kids liked this and knew that she was more interested in letting them write than getting on their case about grammar or writing using proper handwriting. She might actually make a suggestion or provide a youth with a *different way* of writing something. She was very careful to make sure that her suggestions did not sound like insults or put-downs, but came across as an alternative way of doing things. This teacher was more concerned about what they were writing than their ability to write it in standard formal English. She did not get upset easily or lose her temper. She walked around the room slowly and helped each student or asked questions of them. She even liked the fact that I wanted to help and encouraged me to do more than sit in the back of the room and babysit. As I said, for me this class was fun. This day she asked the kids to describe a scene from their lives when they felt safe. The kids looked at her like she was from another planet. She just kept explaining it in different ways until all the kids were writing.

I enjoyed working with her, but she was convinced that it was not the kids' fault they were in trouble. She blamed society or their parents, but never the kids. Occasionally, this attitude would show through in the way she read the kids' writings. I just sat there and let her teach her class. She knew I disagreed with her opinions about societal responsibility. I also knew that this was her class and that we had to work together. It was not my place to point out to her that each of these kids made the choices which landed them in trouble in the first place. Besides, since it was her classroom, I was not going to question her authority in any way, especially in front of the kids.

After a few minutes she and I started to walk around the room. We looked at all the papers to see if there was writing or just tagging on them. Those who had at least half of their page with writing were bound to get praise. There were times I felt she was complimenting a kid more for creative spelling than creative writing. She felt very strongly about the need for a positive atmosphere and I just reminded myself that this was her class and that I was a tolerated guest. Besides, helping the kids was more interesting than working on any of my own personal writing projects.

I was more particular about the kids' grammar and vocabulary. I would look at what they were writing and would try to give them more accurate ways to say things. Some of the kids took my suggestions, and others ignored me. That was OK, because at least they were writing. When I came across a student who had nothing on the page, I would ask him a few leading questions. When they would try to get out of working by claiming that the assignment did not apply to them, I would ask, "You mean you never felt safe during your whole life?" Sooner or later I knew I could pull an answer out of them. Once they started writing, I would go away, which was really what we both wanted.

This is the way the class went for fifty minutes. Once the kids were working independently, I could either work in my journal or monitor the kids. Very occasionally, a youth would ask how to spell something. Five minutes before the class was supposed to end, the students started to ask how soon until they could leave. Just once, I would like to be ready to leave and have the kids look up at me in surprise at how quickly the time had passed.

When the class actually ended, we went to Interpersonal Skills. This class usually went fairly well. The teacher, Diana, came from the same background as the kids. She spent her time trying to give the youths a healthy dose of reality.

Every once in a while, Diana would sit the class down and teach them about the basics of family budgeting. She would start by assuming that they could make a reasonable salary for a high school dropout (around $8.00 an hour). She would then subtract rent, utilities, transportation and other expected expenses. Usually when she hit -$50.00, one of the kids asked about money for clothes, for a date, or for fun. Then one of the kids would yell from the back that they would apply for welfare. She took great pride in demonstrating that when one applies for welfare, they cannot make above a certain amount of money, must be disabled or have screaming babies. She then showed them how much they could make on welfare, and what their expenses would be with this source of income. Each youth offered a way to try to cheat and avoid actually working. Finally, she explained that the only way to live the way they wanted to was by getting vocational training or at least an AA degree. She took great pains to point out that even a G.E.D. will not make it in this day and age. She explained that one must make at least $12 to $14 an hour to make ends meet. Sooner or later a kid would pipe up with the belief that he could make more money selling drugs than he would ever make working.

Diana relished explaining how much they could actually make by selling drugs. She would take the total drug income they could make in a year and divide it by the number of hours they would have to spend in jail for selling when caught. At least one kid would mouth off with, "Then, I just won't get caught." All she had to do was remind them that they were already in detention this time, that this was their fourth time in detention, and that they were surrounded by others who were also caught and in detention. This usually quieted all of the other protesters. In this manner she demonstrated that the average drug dealer actually makes only about $1.14 an hour (based on $10,000/365 days times twenty-four hours). She then reminded them of the shortened life expectancy of many drug dealers. Still, there was always one kid in the back of the room who boasted that he would never get caught again. Diana would then ask, "You mean, like you did not get caught this time, the last time and the time before that?"

After this class, the residents were more ready for third period, Job Finding Skills. Usually the teacher made the class interesting, but the important lessons seemed to go over their heads. These kids could not see themselves working in the real world. Truth be told, most of these kids never desired to hold down even a part-time job. For some of them, the idea of actually holding a full-time, semi-skilled job was as alien an idea as a holiday in Zimbabwe.

While job searches could have been very boring for my residents, the instructor Jonathan made an effort to make it as interesting as possible. He brought in videos and activities. Jonathan offered to type professional resumes for any of the residents as long as they provided him with the necessary information. He tried to avoid teaching theory and used many real-life specific examples to which the kids might relate. In the end, the only thing that kept his class interesting was the fact that the instructor actually cared and had a warped sense of humor; otherwise it would have been a complete waste of everyone's time.

When this class finally ended our day in school was complete. I do not know how much anyone actually expected these kids to learn in a three-hour school day, but the state says that these youths must be in school, so they went to school for three hours. I could now collect my residents and return to the juvenile home. I had to admit that I always felt relieved getting back through that door of the facility with all of the kids. The minute I finished the last pat-down meant the rest of the day would go easier. From now on all I had to do was back up my fellow staff members. In three hours, I would be on my way home. That is, until I remembered that I volunteered to work an additional eight-hour day.

ADDITIONAL INFORMATION

Intervention

You are sitting in the TV room, when two of the youths under your supervision start to talk about the sexual body parts of one of the characters on the program. You have to decide if you are going to intervene in the conversation and if so, how. This is one of the decisions you will make every day as a youth worker. To answer this question you need to know yourself, know your program, and the youths with whom you are working.

Your personality will be the major factor in how much you intervene in youth activities. Your first response will be an emotional one, based on your own personality, gender, and morals. If you are not offended by the comments, you might be tempted to let the conversation continue until you are offended. However, this is not appropriate. An emotional response will teach the youths how to set you off emotionally and thus they will learn ways to control you. Stop before you react, consider the context and the framework of the program in which you are working.

The more controlled your program, the quicker you will need to respond to this conversation. In a "boot camp" type program, this conversation should be ended, right as it starts. A completely controlled model will have rules about such conversations. A program based on individual responsibility might permit you to intervene, but you will need to do this in a manner that puts the responsibility back on the youths. Interventions can include comments like the following: "Is that really an appropriate thing to say?" or "Would you want your mother to hear you say that?" For methods which are appropriate in your program, watch how the more senior staff deals with similar situations and adapt their methods to your personality.

Finally, you need to know the personalities of the youths with whom you are working. With a younger youth, say twelve, you might use a more parental tone, "You don't talk like that around here!" This might not work as well with a seventeen-year-old with a chip on his shoulder. In this situation you might not use a command but rather a suggestion or applied hint: "You do know we don't talk like that around here? Thank you." This gives the youth a chance to correct themselves and save some face in front of their friends.

Personality Conflicts

Do you remember when you were in grade school? You may have had a teacher who was your favorite. He or she taught you well, and you liked going to this class. However, your best friend could not stand that teacher and preferred a teacher who drove you crazy. It is the same way with these high-risk youths. There are some teachers or youth counselors that each youth can work with, while they have problems with others. Do not think you are a failure just because one individual or a group of youths cannot work with you. Remember the youths who can work with you and make what you do worth their time. Also, the client who refuses to work with you today may tomorrow insist on only working with you.

Challenging

The current emphasis on setting higher objectives for youths also includes those in high-risk programs. They are still expected to take the mandatory exams and pass them. Once a youth leaves a program, the world will not give them any special breaks just because they were in detention or needed special help. In fact, the world will make it harder for them to succeed. They will have to prove to any employer that they can be trusted handling money, supplies and expensive equipment. If a youth does not have an employment history, then an employer will look at the kid's school records. A history of attending school in detention will not reflect well on the kid's character. This may not appear fair, but it is reality and this is the reality for which we must prepare our youths. Take that chip on their shoulders and the anger behind it, and transform that emotional energy toward setting and meeting higher expectations. Use phrases like, "OK, prove to me that you can do this." Or, "If you are so tough, then this should be easy for you." This is how these youths can be helped to succeed, not by setting goals so low that they achieve nothing by meeting them.

MAJOR POINTS

1) Each youth and teacher is different. This means no one theory or approach will work with all or even most youths. Be prepared to explain ideas and concepts or work with your students in a variety of ways.

2)   Do not be afraid to challenge your clients. Success comes from overcoming failure, not avoiding it.

3)   Never challenge the authority of a coworker in front of the clients. It not only makes you both look weaker, but it also gives the kids a tool to use against both of you.

4)   Keep an open mind about all of your youths. No one is guaranteed to be a failure until they accept that label for themselves.

CLASS ACTIVITIES

Have each student create a lesson that will last five to seven minutes. The purpose of the lesson is to challenge their classmates' view of the world. The next day break the class into groups of five students. Each student will take turns teaching the group their lessons. The group will evaluate each lesson for clarity and impact. At the end of the class, each group will pick the one lesson they received which has the greatest need for work. The group will develop this lesson and create a lesson plan by which the lesson can be taught to the class as a whole. Each group will then present their lesson to the class. The activity will be evaluated by the instructor based on full group participation and the ability of the lesson to challenge the mindset of the students in the class.

Chapter 4
Morality Centered Questions

QUESTIONS TO THINK ABOUT AS YOU READ

1) How much time can you dedicate to youth causes above that demanded by your job? Volunteer once a month? Work on an as-needed basis? Make monetary contributions?

2) Who is responsible when a teenager gets pregnant? How realistic are your moral views when dealing with the reality on the streets? What will be in the best interests of the future child?

3) Are there times when it is appropriate to set aside your own morals for the best interests of your clients? When is this appropriate for you? When is this dangerous to you?

4) Are there times when it is appropriate to violate agency policies? What are the risks of doing this? What is your liability in violating your employer's policies? Do you have the experience and judgment to makes these types of decisions?

READING

Before my first shift ends, I sit and monitor the youths who are watching TV after lunch. I would normally just sit and vegetate, but today I did not want to sit and watch the same reruns I have watched every day for the last month. I noticed my "friend" Curtis was sitting alone in a corner with his eyes focusing on each car as it drove by.

I could tell by the look on his face that Curtis was thinking about something other than the TV show. His face showed a mix of worry and anticipation. On a hunch I got up and went into the office. Checking the visitors' schedule, I found my hunch to be correct. Curtis was expecting a visit from Steve, a local community youth program director.

"Mr. Jones," I yelled from my office. "Come here, please."

Curtis slowly rose from his chair and dragged his feet towards my office. I signaled him to sit down in a chair across from me. "What's bothering you, Curtis?"

"Nothing."

"Well then, why does the expression on your face remind me of a dead fish?"

"Man, I don't look that bad . . . do I?"

"Do you really want to look in a mirror?" I paused for a moment, before asking, "Does your expected visit with Steve have anything to do with your current mood?"

"Yeah, I guess it does."

"Why does it bother you so badly? What does this Steve do with you anyway?"

"Steve runs the club that I hung out in. Man, he is the only adult who I can trust. I promised him that I wouldn't get into any more trouble."

"You think he is going to be angry with you?'

"Man, you just don't understand. Steve is a man you don't lie to. He's got these eyes that look right through you. When he gets angry, his voice gets low and quiet. You just wish you could melt into the floor instead of sittin' there and haven to listen to him go off."

"Are you afraid he might hurt you?"

"No way. . . I have never even seen him lose control when dealing with anyone. I can't explain it man, but if you know him, you just don't want to let him down, no way, no how."

"Why do you give this man so much respect?" I asked in what had to seem like a stupid question.

"Man, it is hard to describe him. Steve works a night job so that he can keep his center open. Every cent he makes goes into that place. He gives us a place to hang out, as long as we play by his rules and don't do anything stupid. He's cool. He will stay late, or meet with you on your own time. He is the only one I've ever met who has not tried to pull a fast one on me."

The front door rang. I looked up and saw a man who appeared taller than he probably actually was. I asked Curtis to leave the office so I could lock it. As I opened the door, I was greeted by a friendly but confident smile. I knew from Curtis's description and a past visit that this had to be Steve.

"I am Steve. I have come to visit that young man hiding behind you now, Mr. Curtis Jones."

His voice was even deeper than I had expected. When he spoke you could feel the skeleton vibrating inside your body. I began to understand why Curtis had such respect for this man. I invited him in and showed him where he needed to sign the visitors' log.

This was the opportunity I needed to look this "giant" over. Steve had a presence that could fill a major sports arena. He was only five foot nine, but with his broad shoulders, straight back, and penetrating dark brown eyes it was clear to me that he would have no problems controlling even the most difficult of youths. His voice was so deep that I could not help but wonder if it started in an underground cave. He wore a worn pair of jeans with no holes in them, and a plaid shirt with a collar, but no tie. On his feet was a pair of work boots that appeared have been used during at least one world war. He was clearly not a man that anyone would want to make angry.

I invited Curtis and Steve to move into the kitchen where they might have a more comfortable conversation. As we went through the living room, I explained that a staff member was required to be present during all visitations. Steve nodded his head. "I've been here before. I can work with your rules." He was more interested in who was in our living room. The moment I stopped explaining the rules, he was starting to give hellos to many of the youths in the living room. It seemed that he knew most of our residents, and had news about each of their families.

Finally, I got Steve and Curtis into the kitchen. Curtis started to lean back in his white plastic chair, bending the back legs. He looked over at me and saw my glance of disapproval, and slowly put all four legs of the chair on the floor. "Yo Steve! What brings you here?"

"I'm glad you asked!" Steve responded in a tone which indicated he was not really happy to be here at all. "Before you got locked up, were you going out with Melee Brown?"

"Yeah, so?" Curtis's voice was beginning to show some tension. His tight face control showed how he was trying to hide his real emotions.

"She came into the center the other day. She was looking for you everywhere. So I called your mother and found out you were down here...again."

"How is she doing?" Curtis asked. I could tell from the expression on his face that he was not as calm as he wanted us to believe.

"Pregnant!" Steve answered calm but bluntly. He dropped the word like a knife hitting the floor.

After a long moment's pause, Curtis responded, "Yeah, so?" trying not to lose what little emotional control he had.

"So, in seven months you are going to be a father," Steve started. "This means a great deal of responsibility."

Curtis's wall of control broke. "It don't mean nothin'. She knew that she could get pregnant, and she knew she should do somethin' about it. It ain't my problem. If she wants to have a child, that be her problem. I ain't got nothin' to do with it."

"That is not going to be how the court sees it, Mr. Curtis Jones," Steve continued. His voice was getting deeper and more controlled. "They will determine that the child is half your responsibility, and will demand that you pay for half of the child's upbringing. If you refuse to pay, the courts will order your employer to hold back *all* of the money that you owe; even if it means your entire check."

"That's O.K.," Curtis started to rationalize. "They ain't ever going to catch me."

"Like they did not catch you this time, Mr. Jones? They will catch you, and I will help. I am not pleased that you would abandon the young lady you were telling me such wonderful things about just a month ago, just because *you* did not take responsibility for your own actions. I'm also not pleased with this attitude of yours at all." Steve was sitting tall and looking down on Curtis. His voice was low, controlled, echoed around the room, and made me feel cold to my bones. "I am also not pleased that you would abandon your own child the same way your father abandoned you. *DO YOU WANT A CHILD TO THINK THE SAME OF YOU, AS YOU DO OF YOUR OWN FATHER?*" Steve had not raised his voice one bit, but it was so crisp that you could hear the crackling even at my end of the table.

I looked over at Curtis, and could tell he was shaking. This was what he feared. This is why this visit had worried him. He had known all along why Steve was coming, and facing the truth was much harder for Curtis than facing the law. All Curtis could say was, "No, sir."

Deep down inside I have to admit feeling some gratification watching the same Curtis Jones, who had not four days earlier refused to do his chores, now feeling intimidated by nothing more than a man who had the courage to get involved, and who Curtis both respected and feared at the same time.

"Good. I wanted to see if you still had the capability of becoming a man." Steve sat back in his chair. "So what are you going to do about it?"

"I guess that I'm going to have to get a job when I get out, and start taking care of her."

"Actually, you probably should do that anyway, but not because you are going to be a father. Fortunately for you, Ms. Brown has more sense than you, and realized that she was not ready to be a mother. She came to the center looking for you, because she needed the money to terminate the pregnancy."

"She had an abortion! Man. Why did you come in here and scare me like that?"

"Curtis, I want you to start thinking about what responsibilities your own actions *WILL* cost you in the future. You are lucky. I gave her the money she needed, and she has already gone to the clinic to deal with it. I want you to know I was not happy about this. I do not approve of abortions as a replacement for responsibility. It was not for your benefit I gave her the money, but for the child's. She admitted that she is still smoking and using drugs. She did not think she could stop, even for the sake of the child. That is why I gave her the money; not to save YOU from your responsibility. You are just lucky that I am not going to take the money out of your hide in court. I AM, however, going to demand that you work in the center doing custodial work, at minimum wage, until I have been paid back for taking care of your responsibilities. Do you understand, Mr. Jones?"

"Yes! Yes, sir," said a much relieved Curtis Jones. "Thank you, sir."

"Good, now that is taken care of; how are you doing, Mr. Jones?" Steve's voice relaxed and with it the tension in the air seemed to melt away. From the last five minutes I began to understand why so many of our residents knew and respected Steve and the work that he did. This was a man who could pick his battles with these kids so that they could both win.

"I'm doin' O.K., man." Curtis was noticeably more relaxed than he was a few moments ago.

"Are you staying out of trouble, Mr. Jones?" Steve asked.

"Of course, man. What kind of trouble do you think I can get into here . . .?" Curtis cut off his sentence midway when he noticed that Steve was not looking at him, but rather at the raised eyebrow over my right eye.

"Would you like to change your story, Mr. Jones?" Steve asked after a painful pause in the conversation.

"Well, I did have a few problems with the new staff when I got here, but I think he and I have worked things out. Right, man?" It was obvious that I was no longer just an observer in this conversation.

"I hope so. Mr. Jones had a few problems with his temper a few days ago; but once he and I started to talk in private, we were able to address the problems and solve them. Since then, we have learned a working respect for each other."

Steve took his conversation back to Curtis. "What kind of problems have you had?" Steve's voice started to add a more caring tone.

"Beyond the usual things, man, a social worker came by yesterday. She wanted to separate me from Mom and put me in a foster home. I tried to talk her out of that crazy idea."

I sat there and listened to Curtis as he talked to Steve. I noticed that Curtis's speech was improving. I began to realize that Curtis could speak proper English if he wanted to, and if he thought it was to his benefit or gain.

Steve suddenly changed the subject. "I spoke with your mother yesterday."

"What she have to say fo' herself?"

"She called me because she wanted to get the truth out of you. What were you doing with that cell phone? She knows that it was not yours."

"Man, everyone needs a PDA today. It is how I keep in contact with my friends. Everyone is using one today. Besides, the guy I got it from has got plenty of money. It ain't gonna cost him much to replace it. He probably has a new one already."

I realized that this was not the same story he had told me earlier. However, rather than speaking up now, I wanted to hear this new version, so I stayed silent and let Curtis continue.

"Curtis, do you remember when you were eight years old and someone took the money your mother gave you?" Steve started in.

"Yeah, what does that have to do with anything?"

"I also remember that. You came to me crying about what you were going to do. Your mother had trusted you with five dollars, to go to the store and buy some things."

"Yes, I remember, you gave me five dollars and told me not to worry about it," Curtis responded.

"Well, I knew who took the money by the way you described him to me. I saw him that afternoon as he came into the center to play pool. I asked him about it. At first he lied and said that he had not taken it. I told him to tell the truth or I would have you come in and tell me in front of his mother that it was him who took your money. He finally admitted that he had taken the money from you. His excuse was that he knew that your mother had a job and he 'knew that you could just get the money back from your mother anytime'. I told him where you had gotten the money from, and I took the five dollars from him."

"Yeah, so? You got your money back though."

"CURTIS, when will you learn that you cannot judge another person's needs? Only GOD can judge what one person deserves or does not, needs or not, has or not! Are you God, Mr. Jones!?" Steve's voice had gotten deep and cold. The air in the room was still.

I realized that I was at ground zero, and all I could do was wait to see if there was going to be a blast or a dud. Steve was also waiting to see what Curtis was going to do. It was clear that Curtis was thinking. His two realities were clashing, and it showed on his face. Was he going to continue to work with Steve and have a safe place to hang with a father figure he could depend on, or was he about to tell Steve off? The answer was short in coming.

"How dare you accuse me of acting like God? You are the one sitting here judging me. I do what I have to, and I did not ask you to come here and talk to me like my mother! I don't have to stay here and listen to this shit." Curtis got up from his chair and threw it across the floor and stormed out of the room. I heard his stomping feet going into the TV room to join the other youths.

The room was silent for some time. Finally, I could not stand it any longer and said, "I'm sorry it didn't work out, Steve."

"Oh, don't worry about it. If this is anything like the last five times, he will call me at home later tonight and apologize. The only thing which scares me is when they don't call me back." Steve's voice trailed off, but his eyes showed that his mind was elsewhere.

After a few moments of silence I had to ask, "What happens when they don't call back? Do you think you have lost their trust?" I asked naively, hoping to get some insight into this man and his skills.

"Not only have I lost their trust, but in most cases, within one year I have to attend another funeral." Steve's eyes were almost glazed over. He was remembering funerals that he had attended or friends he had lost to failure, prison and the grave. "I can remember the face of each friend I have had to carry to his grave. Each one feels different with their weight on your shoulders that one last time. Each one cannot be forgotten."

We sat in the room quietly for a few minutes. I did not feel comfortable leaving this guest alone when he was obviously disturbed. I knew that my coworker was watching the other youths, and I felt I could sit here for a moment or two and recover after the blast. Besides, Steve had given me a lot to think about.

I was starting to get up from my chair when there was a knock at the doorway. It was Curtis.

"Josh, could you please leave me and Steve alone for a moment?"

I started to get up and leave, but there was a large firm hand on my shoulder.

"Curtis," Steve started. "It's O.K. to talk to me with him here. Nothing said here will leave this room without your permission. Is that correct, Josh?"

"For the most part, yes. If anything must leave this room, I will let both of you know."

"Nothing against you Josh, but I just want to talk to Steve alone."

"I have to stay here, Curtis," I said, "but if it will make you feel any better

I'll go sit in a corner and you can pretend I am not here."

This almost satisfied Curtis. He slowly walked into the room, and went to pick up the chair he had been sitting in just a few minutes earlier and that he had thrown across the room. As he came back to the table, I moved across the room, and my thoughts turned to other things. Every once in a while I looked over at the table where the two men sat and quietly talked. After about five minutes it was clear that the apology was over and Steve was patting Curtis on the back.

After about twenty minutes, the conversation came to a close. Curtis got up and put his chair back where it belonged. He shook hands with Steve and walked out of the room and headed upstairs, as it was now quiet time and all the other residents were in their rooms. Steve turned to thank me, and ask if he could use the restroom.

After he was done, he came to the office to sign out. I documented in the log that he was leaving, and asked him if he got his "phone call."

"One more time, I have been able to reach him. I just don't know for how much longer. It is getting harder and harder to reach that boy. One of these days I am going to lose him."

I just shook my head and let Steve out the front door, a real man.

ADDITIONAL INFORMATION

Cost of Youth Programs vs. Juvenile Detention

Youth programs can range in costs from a few thousand dollars to a few hundred thousand. These costs vary by the size of the program, the number of employees vs. volunteers, and the total others charge for the program's expenses. A middle ground example is the youth program which follows. The annual budget is only $20,000 to $24,000. The program offers an afternoon drop-in program with a few side programs. The facility is rented for a little more than $100 a month. This is really more of a donation to the program, since the rent barely covers the expenses the landlord must pay each month. While the director is only paid for part-time work, he or she commits to full-time demands. For the occasional evening programs, college students volunteer in trade for college credits, experience and something to put on their resume.

The benefits of these programs are surprising, given their low costs. These programs provide supervised youth activities as an alternative to youths getting in trouble. While it is difficult to measure the long-term success of these programs, youths involved in supervised activities are much less likely to get into trouble.

However, these programs require directors who are special people. A youth program director must to be willing to work for less money than a person working in the business community in an equivalent position. These directors have to be able to recruit, motivate, and monitor numerous volunteers. They also have to be willing to deal with youths who can be hostile, manipulative, or even violent.

These people understand that sometimes a youth needs to hear what can be difficult or impossible for a friend or relative to say. A good youth director understands that sometimes when a youth comes to them it is because the youth is already in trouble. They need to point out that it was the youth's own actions which created the trouble and that it is the youth who must solve the problem. This can mean telling the youth things they do not want to or are unwilling to hear. In the story, Steve risks his friendship and working relationship with Curtis, in an effort to challenge Curtis to grow. Steve does this not by using friendly comforting words, but rather by showing Curtis that he was acting like the people he hated most, his own father. Encouraging personal growth is one of the most difficult and rewarding parts of working in a youth outreach program.

However, these people continue to do these jobs for the non-monetary rewards. People who successfully operate or work in youth programs have more than just a passion for the job. Passion can only drive a person for so long before that person burns out. The type of person who will succeed has a long-term drive which pushes them from within. Many of these program directors have troubled pasts themselves, have gotten beyond these problems, and now want to help others. Other youth directors are retired military or police who want to make a direct difference in the lives of these youths. What these people get in trade for their efforts is an opportunity to watch youths grow and change. After all, the real difference between a youth gang and a youth group is appropriate adult supervision.

Detention

Once youths do get into serious legal trouble, they will most likely find themselves in a juvenile detention program. These programs are very expensive. A 12 bed program like the one described in this book annually costs over $600,000 per year. This amount only covered the cost of having two full-time employees on staff 24 hours a day, a drug counselor, supervisor, and food for the residents. These costs average out to about $50,000 per kid per year, and this was considered an inexpensive program, since the building was already owned by the company, and the company was already paying for utilities, insurance, and supplies for their other programs. However, juvenile detention is a necessary part of the law.

The success of juvenile detention is poor regardless of how the programs are evaluated. If juvenile detention is evaluated on the youths not re-offending after release, then the best standard detention programs only have a 20 to 35 percent success rate. Actual numbers vary from program to program; since client files are not centrally organized and are sealed from public disclosure, accurate numbers are difficult to obtain. If juvenile detention is supposed to punish youths for their offenses, then these programs also fail because of the short sentences the youths receive, and the fact that most kids view these detention programs as a joke. Finally, if programs are evaluated based on their keeping the most dangerous youths off the street and out of trouble, they fail because they only work for the time the youth is in detention and at a cost over ten times of those other youth activities.

In short, youth activity programs are much cheaper than juvenile detention. For the cost of one juvenile detention, five to seven youth programs could be operated. Multiple youth programs give youths the best possibility for keeping out of trouble with the law. If a youth does not like one program, he or she can always use other ones with different staff and different activities. Juvenile detention is a necessary program, but it should be used only with those youths that absolutely need long-term confinement. Short-term confinement often only teaches young offenders how to commit more serious offenses when they are released.

MAJOR POINTS
1)   Youth Outreach programs are less expensive and have a better chance for success than detention programs.
2)   Working with high-risk youth is more than just a job. Youths can tell when you are only doing what is required. If they believe you are doing this just for the money, this will make your efforts much less effective. But remember, the clients have to figure out for themselves that you care. THE EXAMPLES YOU SET ARE THE LESSONS YOU ARE TEACHING!

CLASS ACTIVITIES
1)   Each student in class will write a grant proposal to fund an activity for a local youth agency. Students must address who the target of the program will be, what the programs goals are, how the program will reach these goals, and how much the program will cost. Costs must include salaries, location, furnishings, programming, activities, and supplies as overhead.
2)   Break students into groups of five. Each student will take turns presenting their proposal to the group verbally. The group should ask the presenter questions as if they as a committee were deciding whether to fund this program

and at what financial level.

3)   Each student will take the feedback they have received from their group and rewrite their proposal before submitting it to the instructor for grading.

Chapter 5
Welcome to the Hell Complaint Line. Please take a number…and wait.

QUESTIONS TO THINK ABOUT AS YOU READ

1)   How good are you at detail oriented work? How will this affect the type of work you will be qualified to do? How is the quality of your work affected by high levels of stress?

2)   How good are you at observing behaviors in others? Can you tell when someone is trying to hide something? Can you tell when someone is trying to distract you from what others are doing?

3)   How well do you deal with someone who is not behaving rationally when they are your clients, coworkers or supervisor?

4)   How do you react to overwhelming confrontation from groups or individuals?

READING

It was later that afternoon, just before the beginning of my second shift, that my day went to hell. It was 1530 hours and time for me to walk the block to the main secured detention facility. I actually looked forward to these walks as it got me out of the house for a few minutes. Since the main detention facility was so close it made no sense to take a car, even on those days when it was pouring rain. The detainees were supposedly sent to us because they had earned the right to come based on good behavior. It only took two days for me to learn the actual reason that they were sending us these particular youths: the main detention facility was overcrowded, and they needed every extra bed they could get or use. In other words, I learned to expect they might send us anyone.

Entering the main detention facility was easy. Just past the front door, everyone passed through a metal detector that always sounded an alarm. The security guards would give me a quick glance. Since I looked like I knew where I was going, and I was old enough not to be a client, they assumed that I belonged in the building and left me alone. Then I took an elevator downstairs to the detention area. Again, most visitors were required to go through another higher intensity metal detector. If the staff recognized me, they would let me in without even bothering to check to see what I was carrying. If it was a new staffer in the control room, I only needed to explain that they had a copy of my photo-identification in a box on their desk. After that, they usually quit distrusting me and just started to harass me. Once I was let into the security "air-lock," they had to completely close it behind me before they would open the second door to release me into the main facility. This was where they loved to harass me the most, since I had no way to escape, except to give them as much grief right back to them.

Once past security, it was an easy walk down the hall to intake/screening. There I had to wait at yet another secured door, until someone at the security panel looked at the video display, identified me and unlocked the door.

Intake was made up of a number of smaller rooms surrounding a control area in the middle that resembled a "fish tank" looking out into these different areas. At the far end, was a wing of individual cells where new inmates were told to change into uniforms. On the other side of the fish tank was the holding room. Usually there was a mix of males and females in holding, watching TV, sharing stories about scrapes with the law, each trying to "one up" the other, or at least get each other's phone number and a date. The room at the far end was where new inmates would arrive with the arresting or transporting officers. There was another metal detector, a desk and a collection of various forms.

Arriving in the control area, I was greeted by the usual cheery welcome: "What do YOU want?" Rather than taking this abrupt greeting personally, I just gave my usual response: "I want to win the lottery, but since that has yet to happen, I thought I would come here and pick up a juvenile delinquent to bother me for the rest of the night." I had no idea how right I was.

As usual, there were files and paperwork waiting for me on the desk. I had to inventory all of the youth's possessions I was taking with me, and sign for each of them. I quickly glanced through his file to find out if he had a school pass or other complications. Then I needed to verify that I collected all of his medications and my paperwork. His things went into a paper bag; I grabbed the kid's intake photo and then I went to collect the kid.

"Max Smith, you're with me," I called into the holding cell. A large male rose from his chair. It was clear from the way he carried himself that this was not going to be an easy day. He walked up to me and asked, "What da you want?"

"What is your birthday?" I asked him, to verify that this was the youth I was supposed to take with me. He, in turn, mumbled off his birthdate, and unfortunately, it matched. I told him to come with me and we started to walk out through security. I gave his picture to the guards at the double secured doors to show that I was removing an inmate with permission. Once we were on our way, I started the orientation process for the house.

"Welcome to Clarence Seymour House. While at our facility, you will be required to follow all staff directions, and assist with the upkeep of the facility." I stopped my rehearsed speech when I heard mumbling behind me coming from Mr. Smith: "Not if I escape."

I heard this line so many times already that I could give off the standard line without even thinking about it. "That's fine. You will find the front door is unlocked, and when the police catch you again for whatever else you do, you will be charged with escape. Escape carries a mandatory sentence of at least thirty additional days, plus your old sentence with no good time. According to your file you are scheduled to be with us for fourteen days. Do yourself a favor: serve the fourteen, and get out. But if you feel you must make your life complicated, please remember the front door is unlocked. You do not need to use a second floor window and a tree. It is really sad when I need to call an ambulance for an escapee, and we get really upset if you hurt our trees during your daring escape." A quick look at Max showed that he did not even understand I was more concerned about the tree than his safety.

As we arrive back at the house, I directed Max Smith into the main office where I performed a standard pat-down. It was standard procedure specifically written into the manual, and it was almost standard procedure for the youths to accuse the male staff members of being gay, and the female staff of enjoying the process. Once the pat down was completed, reading of the rules would commence. This usually took 45 minutes and was constantly interrupted by either the new resident failing to pay attention, or by other office considerations.

At 1700 hours the orientation was completed. Max succeeded in signing all of the required paperwork. He signed to show that he had had the rules explained to him, and he also showed that he had no intention of obeying any of them. So far I needed to tell him two times to remove his feet from my desk; three times to keep his hands off things on my desk; and five times to repeat what I had just said. He just gave me a blank stare that revealed that he had no idea what I was talking about, nor did he care. I would have discussed this client with my boss if I had not seen her leaving the facility for the day, halfway through the orientation.

Before I let him leave the office, I made a point of carefully examining his face and body language. Every time I got him to sit up straight, his body went right back into a slouching position. His eyes were only half open and were clearly bloodshot. He looked like he wanted to fall asleep, even though it was only five in the evening. I realized that I would need to tell my fellow staff member that this kid was most likely under the influence of something.

While I had been orienting our new resident, my fellow staff member was supervising the youths' rest period up stairs, and was getting dinner set up down stairs. The staff always found it interesting when their job description told them to be in two places at once. With dinner ready and Max oriented, we were ready to get the rest of the residents and serve dinner.

Dinner was accompanied by the usual comments about how terrible the food was compared to the main detention facility or the food at home. The youths also tried to re-establish the pecking order now that there was a new arrival. It was clear from the beginning that all of the youths did not want to mess with Max, and in less than ten minutes it was clear to everybody that he was the top dog of this pack for now. As staff, we tried to keep this from meaning anything, but it is impossible for two staff members to watch twelve clients all of the time. There was always a chance for one youth to take a swing at another without the staff being right there to stop it.

After dinner, we began the chores. Each youth was assigned at least one chore. Since Max was new, he was assigned only one simple chore, sweeping and mopping the floor. This was one simple chore that Max made clear he was going to refuse to do. He wanted to make sure that everyone understood that this was going to be his program to run as he wanted.

I had a different idea. Since he refused to do his chores, I refused to turn on the TV for the other youths to watch. This was one of the ways we tried to use peer pressure to get the kids to do what we wanted. However, instead of doing the floor, Max went over and turned the TV on himself. As I watched him do this, I turned the TV off using the remote control.

I explained to Max that the only way he was going to get to watch TV was by mopping the kitchen floor. I was prepared for him to lose his temper. I was prepared for him to yell at me. I was even prepared for him to threaten me, but instead Max just started to pick up the heavy oak framed furniture and threw it around the room and a few pieces in my general direction.

My main goal went instantly from getting Max to do his one chore, to safeguarding my other residents. "Everyone go up to your rooms. Now!" I yelled. My coworker John was standing by the stairs waiting to help encourage the youths to their rooms and to make sure that Max did not follow them up the stairs. Max made it clear that he had other plans. "I will kill anyone who leaves this room." For a moment there was silence. Everyone waited to see who would make the first move.

To my surprise it was Curtis Jones who stood up and started to move toward the stairs. I did not know or care if he was acting out of obedience or self- preservation, but everyone else started to follow him. John made sure that everyone followed, while I made sure that Max was separated from the rest of the youths. I placed myself between this temper storm and the rest of our clients. He continued to threaten everyone as they moved away from him, and their refusal to listen to him only made him angrier. He resumed his actions of throwing furniture around, and then went into the kitchen to do more damage.

Since I was not physically able to stop him, nor was I permitted to use restraints (rope, chains, hand cuffs or leg irons), I called my boss to let her know what was going on. "Call the police!" she told me, asking why I had even bothered to call her. At that moment I was a little too concerned to explain that the policy manual she wrote directed the staff to call her first during any major incident. So I called 911. As I explained to the operator where I was and what I did, Max, still huffing and puffing after his exertion in the kitchen, came in and sat down in a chair across from my desk. The kid was actually surprised when he discovered that I was calling for the police to come and arrest him.

Now, I knew that the nearest police station was only two miles away, and that the nearest patrol car was only two minutes away. However, I also knew that it would take at least fifteen minutes for any of them to actually show up. Past experience had taught me that they would rather let the kid escape or the situation solve itself. Now, to my surprise, Max stopped hyperventilating, calmed down, and sat down in a chair across the desk from me. So for the next fifteen minutes he and I sat in my office discussing what was going on and what was going to happen to him. He was suddenly concerned about getting more charges on his record, and what his parents would think. I knew that he was just trying to avoid the inevitable, but there was no point in getting him angry again when he could easily start throwing me around like the furniture that now littered the living room. So I sat there and calmly dodged questions, and tried to keep a calm conversation going until there was a knock on the front door.

I was hoping that this would be the police, but I was not so lucky. It was Max Smith's mother asking to drop stuff off for her son and asking if she could see him. I explained to her that if she wanted to visit she would have to call ahead and get permission, and that visitations must to take place during scheduled visiting hours. I tried to avoid explaining what had just taken place, as

I did not want to deal with an angry youth and his upset mother.

From behind my back I heard Max's voice. "Mom, he called the cops and is accusing me of breakin' the place up." There went all my hopes for a calm solution to this problem. I had hoped the police would come and get this kid, ask each of us a few questions and take him back to intake where they would find a padded cell for him. But this was not to be.

The same youth whom I had just witnessed tearing furniture apart and throwing heavy objects around the room was now telling his mother that I had done it, and accused me of trying to blame it on him, so he would get in more trouble. One look at his mother's face told me that I was in real trouble. Since I knew that there would be no calm way of explaining to this woman that her son was lying and I had ten other youths who were witnesses, not to mention my coworker, all I could do was try to talk to her down as best I could until the police arrived. No wonder Max had sat in the office calmly; he knew his mother was coming. The five minutes longer it took for the officers to arrive felt like a lifetime. I had a stoned kid behind me and his angry mother in front of me. Both were calling me a racist and threatened to sue me to hell and back. It was all I could do to remember to breathe and not hyperventilate, because my heart was beating so strongly I could feel each pulse in my throat.

Finally, three officers arrived. One officer took each of us and took down our stories. I asked my officer to talk with my coworker to corroborate what I said. She told me that this would not be necessary, as she and her colleagues had plenty of experience dealing with Max and his mother. I was somewhat relieved when I came out of my office, and saw that Max was already in handcuffs. I was happily surprised to see that his mother was also in cuffs. One of the officers explained to me that she had slapped an officer in the face for accusing her son of lying. Further, they found marijuana on her during the pat-down search. The officer suspected that she had brought it to give to Max. It took all of fifteen minutes for the officers to get all of the information that they needed and to give me the case number they would be filing this under. Then they left, leaving me in a quiet house, trying to remember how to breathe, my own name and on what planet I was living.

I then started the long task of documenting everything that had taken place. My coworker, John, let the other youths come downstairs and asked all of them to help him to clean up the mess. I knew that no one else would try anything tonight, as everyone knew that tonight was going to be the wrong night to act up. I filled out an incident report, a log report, damage report, and a youth returned report, and finally I called my boss to let her have a verbal report. She thanked me for letting her know that everything was under control, but made it clear to me that she did not want to have to deal with anything until tomorrow.

My coworker kindly handled all of the youths while I dealt with my stack of paperwork. Once I finished reporting everything, I then had to collect all of Max's personal belongings, including what his mother had just brought, and document that everything was there. I bagged it up, and took it back to the main detention facility. I walked slowly down that hill as I did not want to have to deal with Max if he was still in the intake area.

Sure enough, he was still there. He was locked in one of the isolation/changing cells. He was making it clear to all who would listen that he was not happy. I think he finally stopped pounding on the walls and doors when he broke his fist. He then demanded to be taken to the health clinic to have it looked at. I dropped off his belongings and started the paperwork to log them back in. During this time, I watched as Max was dragged down to the health center in hand and leg cuffs. When he realized I was watching, I got the opportunity to listen to him threaten me at least five more times about what he was going to do to me when he was released or escaped.

After he was gone, I finished my paperwork and stopped for a rest. Technically, I should have hurried back to help my coworker with the rest of the youths, but I was in no hurry tonight. I took an extra five minutes to read part of the newspaper I saw lying around. I needed a mental health break before I was ready to deal with anyone. The last thing I needed to do was to return to my program early while I was still stressed, and bite the head off of some kid who had only asked me for the time of day.

Upon returning to my own facility, I was greeted by ten youths who all wanted to know what had happened to Max. I explained that he and his mother had been taken into custody, and that he broke his hand while slamming it against a brick wall. Only after a few minutes of calm did I call Curtis Jones into my office.

"Thank you for being a positive leader tonight. You took what could have been a bad situation, and turned it around," I told him. He shrugged off my compliments and made it clear to me that he did not want the other youths to think he was a goody-goody. I let him go back, but not before I told him that I would document his good behavior in his file. He walked out of my office, saying over his shoulder, "I really don't care."

The rest of the evening went calmly. The kids watched TV, parents came and visited, and at 2200 hours, all of the kids were in bed and the lights were out. I spent the next half hour documenting the youths' activities in each of their folders. This was the first chance I had to read the fine print of Max Smith's file. The file made it very clear that Max was serving time for a probation violation.

When I finally came to the part where the file said why he was on probation in the first place, I found out that he had been found guilty of Assault One. Assault One is an assault with deadly intent. This kid had shot at a drug enforcement agent five times with a semi-automatic pistol when the officer tried to arrest him for selling illegal drugs. Fortunately, the officer was wearing his flak jacket and ballistic helmet. The officer returned fire, hitting Max three times and putting Max into the hospital for three weeks of recovery from abdominal injuries. Now Max showed off his injuries as a badge of courage to show his homies what he had done. When midnight came, I was very glad to go home in one piece. Max would spend another night in the hospital with a self-inflicted broken hand. I was also pleased that I would not have to come back to work for almost eight hours and that I was not spending the night in the hospital.

ADDITIONAL INFORMATION

Observation

One of the hardest challenges successful youth workers face is to balance their own creativity and energies with the need for detail-oriented work. When working with a population of youths, you will have to constantly stop what you are doing and make sure you know what each youth is doing or write a report. This requires the ability to watch every detail and document every detail. While you are working on one project or with one group of youths, you will need to be able to answer questions about what the other youths are doing.

This type of observation is necessary not only because unsupervised youths can find trouble, but also because youths are constantly testing their pecking order. A pecking order is an informal chain of command with the most respected youth on top. Respect can be earned by bragging, reputation, threats or fights. It is the last two, threats and fights, which youth counselors must watch and stop immediately. While a youth pecking order is natural, it can cause problems when the youths feel their pecking order is above the authority of the staff of your program. Therefore, as a staff member, you will need to keep your eyes out for any sign that a youth pecking order has gone beyond a prestige issue and is a threat to your authority or your program.

Youth establishing a pecking order can be difficult enough for staff, but it is even more difficult when the new youth is still under the effects of drugs or alcohol. If a youth comes into your program with red eyes, is not following directions, shows sudden unpredictable mood changes, and shows signs of potential violence, keep an eye on this kid. These signs alone are dangerous, but they can also indicate drug use. A youth who is coming off the effects of drugs does not belong in an uncontrolled situation. Remember that it is your primary responsibility to protect yourself, followed by the other youths in your supervision. Take whatever steps you can, as directed by your program, to isolate this youth and keep him under control for at least 24 hours.

Another threat that everyone who works with kids needs to watch for is that of mental illness or other mental issues. Observe the newcomer's mood and notice if he shows signs of unstable or constantly changing emotions. Does he appear to be emotionally closed, or refuse to communicate? This can either be a sign of depression or other mental issues. Unfortunately, these same signs can appear with kids of different cultures, so you need to be aware of each client's background. Finally, be aware that there are some mild personality disorders, such as Asperger's syndrome, that can also make it difficult to work with some clients.

To summarize, while you are working on a project or with a specific youth, keep an eye on the details of what others are doing. They could be hiding contraband or challenging the pecking order. Also watch for any signs that someone is under the influence of illegal drugs or alcohol, as these youths are the most likely to challenge the pecking order or your authority, thus placing you and others at risk of injury.

Legal Definitions

Even if you are not an attorney or working directly in the court system, when you are working with high-risk clients, you will need to have a basic understanding of legal terms. These terms are often used by clients and other professionals around you, and you will need this information to be aware of the level of risk from, and needs of, various clients. A clear example of this is the four levels and three types of assault recognized in Washington State Law. The definitions which follow are summaries based on the Washington State Pattern Jury Instructions (West Publishing Company, St. Paul Minnesota, 1994), a book formulated to explain specific legal definitions to people who have been selected to serve on a jury.

The four levels of assault are determined by the amount of harm caused and who was harmed. An Assault One charge requires the intent to inflict serious bodily harm or death, using a firearm, weapon or other method likely to produce great harm or death. Assault Two is similar to Assault One, but does not require the prosecution to prove that the defendant showed intent to cause great bodily harm or death. Assault Three is an assault which occurs under special circumstances, such as to an on-duty police officer or bus driver. Assault Four is any other type of assault and can range from simple unwanted touching to a bar fight or domestic violence.

Within these four levels there are three types of assault in Washington State Law as written in the Revised Code of Washington. The first type of assault is one where the victim is actually harmed or injured. However, someone does not actually touch or shoot someone to be guilty of the various levels of assault. If one attempts to shoot or strike another, but fail, they are still guilty of assault. Further, one can be guilty of assault even if they make another person believe they are going to be injured, even if the defendant did not actually intend to cause injury. An example of this is pointing an unloaded gun at the victim.

Notice how understanding these charges can affect how you will interact with a client who has been charged or convicted of any of these offenses. You might be willing to provide one-on-one counseling unsupervised to a person charged with Assault Four, but you should take extra safety precautions before doing so with a client charged with, or convicted of, Assault One. Remember, you must still offer the same quality of services to the higher-risk client, but you should do so with the concerns of your own safety in mind. Failing to provide services to a defendant who has been charge or convicted of more serious crimes limits your ability to perform your full duties, and, further, it shows the client that you fear them, and thus you start to lose the illusion that you are in control of the situation.

MAJOR POINTS

1) Balance your own approach with the need to follow policies.

2) Always watch for signs of drug use in your clients and trust your instincts.

3) Remember your life is worth protecting. If you are hurt, you cannot protect the youths for which you are responsible. Put your safety first!

CLASS ACTIVITIES

1) Separate the class into groups of five. Four of the students will agree on how they will confront the fifth student to try to do something inappropriate (i.e. go for ice cream when they should be studying). The fifth student will try to convince the other four students to act appropriately. Each student will take a turn being the advocate. After the exercise is over each group should not only discuss what each member felt when they confronted the group, but more importantly, who was the most successful advocate and why. Was their size or gender an issue? Did they carry themselves confidently or timidly? Could their method work for others in the group or could it be adapted?

2) As individuals, reread this chapter. The youth worker made a number of mistakes that could have put him or others in danger. Write a two-page paper listing the mistakes that were made, how these mistakes could put others in

danger, and how they could be prevented. Please notice that there are never perfect ways to handle situations like these, but there are always better ways. The purpose of this exercise is to prepare you to handle just such an event, so keep your improvements appropriate for your own personality.

3)   As an individual or in groups of no more than five people, research the law in your state for one specific charge which has varying degrees of severity (such as theft). Find legal sources for in your state, cite them, and create a presentation which explains in common language the various levels of the offense. Be prepared to answer questions from the class dealing with the effects of these definitions on behaviors, whether they are criminal or not. If the acts are criminal, the group should try to agree as to level, type of crime, and safety concerns they pose to the youth worker.

Chapter 6
Home Court Advantage

QUESTIONS TO THINK ABOUT AS YOU READ
1) What assumptions do you have about the juvenile court system? Who is involved and what do they do? Who is not involved? What procedures do they follow? What are the rights of the accused? What are the rights of the victims?
2) How accountable should a youth worker be for the actions of the clients under his or her supervision? How realistic is this opinion in our modern age?
3) How strong are the relationships between gang members in reality? What causes the strengths and weaknesses of these relationships?

READING

I never liked getting up early for work. 6:30 a.m. always came way too early, especially when I had only four and a half hours of sleep. Fortunately, today was scheduled to be an easy day. I would arrive and take the kids to school. Then we would come back and have lunch. After lunch, I would have to take Curtis to court for a preliminary hearing. In other words, I would spend most of the day sitting around doing nothing difficult, making sure that Curtis also did nothing.

I arrived at work, and was greeted by the usual sarcasm. "Sounds like you had a quiet evening. You rested enough for today?"

"Would it change anything if I said 'no'?" Wanting to change the subject quickly, I asked, "Anything special I need to know about today's schedule?"

"Yeah, you are scheduled to take Mr. Jones to court today."

"That's fine. I don't care to spend more time here than I have to. If I can avoid being called into the boss's office for more than two minutes, I'll be a much happier person. I don't want to explain why two of the chairs are broken and two more are damaged."

"I'll tell Sarah to make sure that the boss reads your reports and the log before you get back from school."

"Thanks, but please make sure that she reads that kid's file. He may have been here on a probation violation, but he was on probation for shooting at a Drug Enforcement Agency officer. That kid was a real winner and should have never been placed in a minimum security facility." Changing the subject, I asked, "O.K., where are the kids?"

"They are just waking up now. Most of them upstairs and everyone else is setting up the kitchen."

I then took a few minutes to read the log and find out what happened after I left. I checked my mailbox; it was empty. Looking at the calendar on the wall, it was clear that the only unusual activity was taking Curtis Jones to his hearing in the afternoon. After breakfast, I started the chore inspection procedure. The kids completed their chores without problems, so the TV was turned on. I was glad to let them watch their 1/2 hour of cartoons before driving them the two blocks to school.

Fortunately for me, school was completely uneventful. They had no substitute teachers, and everyone was prepared for my kids. Not that I had anything against substitute teachers, but I knew that these kids enjoyed finding each person's emotional weak spot and using it against them. The newer the substitute, the worse the kids could be, and the more effort I needed to put forward to control them. Today, I would get to sit back and rest. None of my kids acted out, and a few of them even seriously did their work. I took the opportunity to rest my eyes, though I was careful not to fall asleep or snore. One class followed another and if I was not resting, I was drawing or reading. When it was finally over, I was glad to take these young men back to the house. In the house, we had more control over who these kids were talking to and how they spoke.

When we returned to the house, I was informed that Intake had called with some special information about Max Smith. Last night when he was taken to the hospital for his hand, they ran a drug test. He came up positive for marijuana, crack and trace quantities of other drugs. The fact that I had picked up and worked with a violently stoned kid did not make me feel any better about yesterday. The fact that the boss was told about these test results did please me. This information probably saved me from a long uncomfortable time in my boss's office explaining to her why I was not able to control this one individual by using my "counseling skills."

Since I took the kids to school and supervised them for three hours alone, my coworker got to watch them during lunch while I wrote my required log entries covering the kids' day at school. Once the kids were done with lunch, my rest was over, and I had to help supervise the cleanup.

Finally, 1315 hours arrived. It was time to take Curtis across the street to court. I took one look at the clothes that Curtis was wearing and was dismayed. He was wearing jeans with holes in them and a black T-shirt with a printed marijuana leaf on it. I asked him if that was what he really wanted to wear to court, and all he did was shrug his shoulders. I sent him back up to his room to change into something more appropriate. I might have been surprised by Curtis's choice of clothing if I did not know that the way most of these kids arrive at court would make Curtis look formally attired. When Curtis came back down the stairs, he was still dressed in street clothes, but at least these did not have holes or images guaranteed to anger any judge.

I logged Curtis and myself out of the facility and took him to court. On the walk across the street, Curtis talked a bit about his approaching court hearing. "This is just a case setting; nothing important is actually going to happen. And if David Ross shows up, I should be able to just walk out."

I was somewhat surprised by this comment and decided to question him about it. "What do you mean, if David Ross shows up you will walk?"

"I told you before, I did not steal the PDA. David did. I was holding it for him so the cop would not find it on him. He already pled guilty to taking it, and served his time. He'll show up and *I WILL WALK*." Curtis was confident. I chose not to point out to Curtis that this was the third change he had made to his story in the last week.

If he was talking about the same David Ross that I knew, I expected David would not appear. He had been in our house three weeks ago and was the one kid who was responsible for my baptism of fire. He took great joy in making my first weeks on the job miserable. He challenged my authority every chance he could, without going far enough to get into real trouble or to be returned to the main detention facility. I was almost afraid to ask Curtis, but I had to know: "How do you know David will show up?"

"He's my homie, man. He'll show. We wear the same hang with the same gang; we're brothers. He's come with me in street fights, and I know that he'll show." Curtis was slipping back into street talk and hand movements. I think that was because he was thinking about his life on the street.

I could have pointed out to Curtis that gang members are usually only "brothers" when it is mutually beneficial. I already saw gang members who would go into a fight for each other or risk life and injury on the streets, yet leave their "homies" alone at the court house. On the streets, they may be homies, but there is no real gain for a gang member by backing up bros in court. At least on the streets that kind of support gives a gang member prestige. In the courts, it just gives them more jail time. I kept this idea to myself, because this was not the time to start an argument with Curtis. He was about to face this reality on his own.

Our conversation came to an end as we walked through the courthouse doors. These were the same doors we walked through when we picked the kids up from detention. As soon as we entered the door, Curtis's manner changed completely. He suddenly lowered his head and shoulders, and bent over to conceal his true height. His eyes went from their normal complete intensity to completely withdrawn so quickly that I almost did not see it happening. It was clear to me that he was trying to portray himself as the victim of the system.

We both found our way over to the sign-in table, and then went to sit in the waiting room. The waiting area was actually broken into about six different sitting areas, each separated either by the main walkway or a short glass wall. Attorneys were speed walking up and down the halls looking for someone who looked like their clients. Not that they actually had any idea what their clients looked like. These attorneys were assigned to these cases only a few days ago. I knew that these people were hard working, but at case settings, they could not help but look confused.

In one of their arms each lawyer carried a large stack of the same orange folders with which I worked. Within this chaos there were a very few parents looking for their children. Only one in twenty kids had their parents at court to support them. Detention officials were running around trying to find out when they needed to have which kid in each courtroom. All I had to do was make sure that Curtis did not walk out the door, and if he did that, I was to report it immediately. This was going to be a piece of cake as long as I could keep from falling asleep.

At one end of the room were the security guards and the metal detector. The only ones who actually got stopped there were the parents, kids who were not in detention, and lawyers who did not yet know to ignore the metal detector. Besides, even with all of these security measures, no kid would actually start a fight here. They were too busy trying to look like innocent little children.

After a half an hour of reading the book I brought with me, Curtis and I were finally approached by one of the attorneys. "I am Rob Nelson. I have been assigned to Curtis Jones as his attorney, and you are?"

"I am Josh, from the Clarence Seymour House. I am currently responsible for Mr. Jones," I answered.

"May I please speak with Curtis in one of the conference rooms?" he asked.

"Of course, but I need to stay with him at all times," I answered. Not that I really wanted to listen in, but I was not permitted to let Curtis out of my sight.

Curtis looked at his attorney and gave an expression that he did not care if I was there, so we walked into one of the small conference rooms to the side of the main waiting area. Curtis grabbed a seat while Rob closed the door. I sat off in the corner, and let the two of them talk. Curtis continued to plead his innocence, and Rob listened while he read Curtis's file. Rob made it clear through his questions that he had only had enough time to quickly glance at the file. Fortunately, this was only a case setting hearing, where the ground rules for future hearings are set down. Rob began the formal interview by explaining that he also had three other clients that afternoon, so while it appeared that he was ignoring us, in fact he was just running between his different clients. I had learned during my own internship in a different juvenile court that high caseloads for public defenders were quite normal.

"Have you seen David today?" Rob asked.

"No, but I know he'll show up."

"O.K. then. Let's go over your case," Rob began. He started to read the standard information out of his copy of Curtis's orange file. Curtis just sat there and nodded his head from time to time. Occasionally he gave a vocal answer, but those were only "uh-huhs" and "yeahs."

Rob asked, "This is only a case setting, correct?"

"Yeah."

"Good. If David does not show up, than all we have to do is let the prosecutor argue about whether to continue to hold you pending trial. This means that it might only take about twenty minutes. Unfortunately, your hearing is set for the end of the day."

"Unfortunately," I thought to myself. This meant that I would be able to sit around all afternoon, and I would get paid for it. I probably should have been more concerned about the needs of my coworkers, but after last night, I needed to take some time to remember that all shifts are not like last night.

After ten minutes, Curtis and I were dismissed out into the waiting room. Once again I was free to read my book, while Curtis worked on his innocent appearance. Once in a while I took a look at him, and it appeared that he was almost getting good at it until we were called into court. "Curtis Jones to courtroom Three," the loudspeaker blared in a half understandable static.

As we walked into the courtroom, Curtis's face changed in an instant from innocent to despair. "What's wrong?" I whispered to him.

"The judge knows me. It looks like you will be stuck with me for a while."

Sure enough, before we even found our seats, the judge looked at us and commented, "Mr. Curtis Jones, I thought we had an agreement that you would not appear before my court again, and I would not lock you up, and forget where

I put you?" Curtis only responded by moving his head lower. It was clear by the expression on his face that Curtis was now feeling mighty low. There was nothing I could do, so I took my seat in the back of the room and watched as the prosecutor laid out the basics of her case and asked that Curtis be held for trial. Rob tried to put forward a defense to this request for release conditions, but it became clear quickly that the judge knew Mr. Jones better than his attorney did.

"Mr. Nelson, I respect your considered request on behalf of your client. Unfortunately, Mr. Jones has already shown me that he will not appear in court without either being in detention or being arrested. I do not need to consult the computer to remember the last time Mr. Jones promised to appear, and then I needed to issue a warrant for his arrest. Unfortunately, your client's past behavior before this court is the reason why I will not be setting any release conditions at this time."

Curtis was not happy to be walking back to the house. He had left, bragging to everyone that he would be leaving when he came back after court. Instead he was walking back to where he would be staying for at least two more weeks. I walked in and was welcomed by the coworker who was my relief. He was there for the past half hour and was ready to take my keys and push me out the door. I just put Curtis's new court date on the calendar, signed out on my time sheet, put it in the boss's box, and left for my weekend. Thursday and Friday as a weekend was just another reality of working in a juvenile detention.

ADDITIONAL INFORMATION

Clients and the Courts

To many high-risk youths, the juvenile court system is just a consequence of the life they lead. They do not feel that a visit to court requires any change of clothing or outward appearance. Most youths will not even have their parents at court if they have a choice. The only change that most will make is an outward change in attitude, but even this is almost always an act.

Most youths will wear the same clothes to court that they wear on the streets. During my first internship with one juvenile court, I observed 96 different youths and only four wore clothing appropriate for a formal occasion. The rest of the youths were wearing old jeans and T-shirts. These shirts often were advertisements for beer, cigarettes or had images of illegal drugs. In short, this attire was more to impress the other youths in the courtroom rather than the judge or court officials.

In my experience during three different jobs with different juvenile courts, only five percent of all youths showed up with one or both parents. Recently, the State of Washington changed the law to require parents to appear with their children during court. This change is part of the current movement to make parents more accountable for the actions of their children. As part of this new process, the parents are served with separate subpoenas. This is so the court knows that the parents are aware of the hearing and can hold the parents accountable if they don't appear.

The only noticeable change in these youths during court hearings is in their body language. While I was escorting youths to court, they would often speak defiantly about their situation and the charges against them. The moment they entered the courthouse their backs would slouch, the fire would leave their eyes and the anger would reduce their voices. This act would carry on while they spoke with their public defender and when they entered the courtroom. The youths would only talk with one another briefly so as not to damage facial expressions and body language. In short, youths do not seem to see the courts as a serious threat to their street lives. While in court they may "walk the walk and talk the talk," but they don't even think of changing their clothes to impress a judge.

While studying interactions of youths with the court system, it is necessary to have an understanding of the roles of the active participants. These roles are defined in state law and therefore are different from state to state. The four active participants are usually the judge, prosecutor, defense counsel, and the probation officer.

The judge has the most complex role in the courtroom. During the proceedings, the judge acts as arbitrator of dispute. These disputes range from what the release conditions should be to what evidence can be presented and finally, the appropriate sentence. Sentencing in juvenile cases is complex balance of variables. The sentence is meant to rehabilitate the youth, more than just punish them for the earlier illegal behavior. It is the judge who must make the most difficult decisions. Overall, the judge represents the law and the wishes of the people of the state through the laws.

The role of the prosecutor is to represent the society which has been injured by the breaking of the law. It is the prosecutor's primary job to prepare and present a case that shows that the youth in question broke the law. The prosecutor tries to balance society demands for punishment and its desire to keep the youth from breaking the law in the future.

The defense counselor is an attorney, usually hired by the government directly or through a contract, since most juvenile defendants cannot afford their own attorney. The defense counselor will first try to get the charge dismissed, or failing that, get the best plea bargain he or she can get for the youthful client. Because of the large caseloads that these attorneys carry, they mostly do plea bargains, as they do not have enough time to prepare cases for trial, let alone investigate each case. Even with this limitation on their efforts, most public defense counselors work an average nine- to ten-hour day and do additional work on weekends.

The probation officer or counselor is the research and enforcement arm of the court. The probation officer's job, prescribed by various state laws, is to make sure that youths are following the pre-trial release conditions and sentences ordered by the court. These orders can include required behaviors, community service, treatment, jail time and fines. The probation counselor will try to meet with the youth routinely to make sure the defendant is following these orders and is on schedule to complete any sentencing conditions. These meetings can take place at the youth's home, school, job, jail cell or in the probation office. Because the youths with whom the probation officer works have different schedules, these meetings can take place in the evenings or on the weekends. The reality of a modern juvenile probation officer's job is a very large case load of well over fifty cases at a time. This means that the officer's time is divided between being in court, talking to schools and other community resources, and interviewing youths. This reality limits many probation counselors' abilities to work with individual youths on a regular basis. It also will affect the amount of time they will have to spend with their own families, as unpaid overtime may be a requirement of the job.

In short, every person in the courtroom has a role to play. The law of each state dictates their roles, but the reality of high caseloads greatly affects how effective each person can be in fulfilling them. Many of the people who fill these roles are strong-willed and dedicated, which helps them deal with the pressure and the reality that it takes more than the forty hours they are paid for to complete their job to their own satisfaction.

Relations of Youths in Gangs

Much has been said on the television, in video games and movies about how youths in gangs band together to protect one another. The youths themselves believe and perpetuate this belief. Many of them believe their own families have failed them in some way. They look to the gang to protect them in ways they feel their family cannot or will not. Unfortunately, the reality of gang life and gang protection is not everything these youths try to believe it to be.

The street gangs of today are based on a family model. These youths call each other "bro" or "brother" and expect the other members to look out for their interests like siblings. This use of surrogate family members to fill a person's current needs is an ancient pattern, but these models from other cultures or times usually are based on much stronger family models.

Many gang members come from single-parent families with minimal financial resources. They look to gang membership for protection and friendship. Others join gangs because they believe that their parents don't care for them or understand their needs. Whether this belief is true or not is not an issue to be addressed here. However, because gang members feel their families have failed to meet their needs, and the gang is based on their misunderstanding of how a family works, the youth gang is also likely eventually to fail to meet a youth's perceived needs.

Gangs cannot substitute for a good family. Many times youths will expect the gang to back them up or protect them, but their "gang brothers" will only come to assist when they feel it is in their best interest to come and assist. An example of this behavior was shown in this chapter when Curtis's fellow gang member failed to appear for a court hearing. The other youth had nothing to gain by appearing. In a street fight you support your fellow gang members because that gives you prestige before the group, but helping your "gang brothers" in court does not give you any prestige. Another example of how gangs fail these youths is the fact that you cannot appear weak in front of your fellow gang members, because then they will not respect you. If you yourself publicly question or doubt your own behavior or activities, this is a sign of weakness. However, these are also the behaviors required for personal growth and development. If a youth is not free to ask if what they are doing is right for them, and discuss these questions with their peers and family, then they cannot grow and develop as a person. This is why the youth's beliefs that his or her own family has failed him or her will weaken the bonds he or she will form within the gang.

MAJOR POINTS

1) Juvenile courts are very different from what people expect. In addition, each juvenile court is different from others, even if they are in the same state.
2) Juvenile courts and their employees are usually stretched for resources and workers. Remember that in this line of work, there is always something more people could do if only they had the time and resources.
3) Gang relationships are only as strong as the model they are based on. These relations are not as strong or multifunctional as the youths want to believe.

CLASS ACTIVITIES

1) If the juvenile court in your community is open to the public, go to the court and observe the activities for a minimum of four hours. Watch the people and

try to identify their roles. Compare your observations with the descriptions in this chapter. In class, discuss the differences and the similarities between what you have read and what you witnessed.

2)   If the juvenile court in your community is closed to the public, then invite a prosecutor, public defender and a juvenile probation counselor to come and speak to your class about their careers (please note that court schedules may require that this class session be held at noon or in the evening). Have them explain their jobs to the class. Students will then write a paper on how what the guest described is similar or different from what they read in this book or expected.

Chapter 7
A Walk in the Park

QUESTIONS TO THINK ABOUT AS YOU READ

1) How well do you work within rules and guidelines?
2) How might your personality show in your work?
3) Does your personality allow you to work with different people in different situations?

READING

It was 0630 hours on a Saturday. For anyone else with a normal work schedule it was time for sleeping in and preparing for a day with the family. Many of my friends were planning to work on their houses, do laundry, or just sit and read a book. Unfortunately, for me and many more people in this world, Saturday is just named Monday.

The drive to work would have been uneventful had the road crew not started to rip the road apart. It might not have been so bad, if they had not decided to start in the middle lanes. I had known that they would be doing this, and I left early so that I could avoid being late. I had calculated it just about right, arriving at work at the wonderful hour of 0750.

The bright side of this was that I did not have to wake the kids until 0900. The official schedule said that they were supposed to be awake at 0800, but since the boss was not coming in today, and the residents objected to being woken early, the staff could use the extra time to read up on what we needed to know, complete other assigned duties, or just relax. My coworker chose to take advantage of the time to get in an extra cigarette. On this morning I took extra time to read the program log to see if there was any follow-up to my earlier incident.

It looked like today was going to be a nice day. The kids we had all looked like they would not cause much trouble. The log entries read like the ideal official daily schedule: no riots, no arguments, no kids walking around after lights out to pull pranks. I checked my box and found a note asking me to work another shift next Thursday. This meant an extra $64 in my paycheck, and another 6-day week. I folded the note and put it in my pocket. My wife would be doing classwork in the lab during that shift, so there was no real point in turning it down. Besides, I could use the money to take a "little brother" of mine to a basketball game, or spend it on gifts for the holidays.

After the required reading, I had a half hour to sit and read my newspaper and relax before I woke up my charges. The half-hour went by too quickly and by nine, I had already sent 3 different youths back to their rooms, and I could tell that I was not going to get away with procrastinating any longer. I called Mike in from his last puff of smoke, and I went upstairs to start the day.

I always enjoyed waking them up. All day they would take pleasure treating the staff as if we were their slaves. Waking them up gave me the opportunity to feel the illusion of being in complete control. I was super cheery and happy, and watched as most of the youths woke up grumpy. Many of the youths asked how I could be so joyous this early in the morning. For some reason, these kids could not understand that I had to get up three hours before they did in order to get here and be ready to deal with them.

When I got to Curtis's room, he was already awake and dressed. He was sitting on his bed, legs crossed, and was staring out the window. I said my good mornings to him, and asked if his pre-breakfast chores were done. He only moved his head up and down, but kept his eyes focused outside the window. I asked him if there was anything wrong.

"Nah. I am just stuck in this place for another two weeks. I was hoping to be out of here for my birthday, but I found out yesterday that they are not even going to give me a day pass on Tuesday. I'm going to have to go to school, and do everything just like any other day. My fifteenth birthday will be just like any other day."

"Why do you think they turned down your request for a day pass?" I asked.

"The judge ordered that I have to be held because she says I might not show up in court in two weeks."

"Is there a reason why she might not believe you will show up?"

"No," Curtis snarled.

"Curtis?" I asked trying to prod a more honest answer out of him.

"Well, I did have two warrants out for not coming to court, but I have dealt with them. I mean, they're history, so why do I have to be here on my birthday?"

Had Curtis been like most residents and already convicted, or had pled guilty, I would have told him that he did the crime and now he must do the time. Since Curtis was pre-trial, this easy out would not work. "Curtis, will you remember this birthday?"

"Yeah, as one of the worst I've ever had."

"I think that is why the judge gave her order. She might believe that if you remember what it is like to be in jail on your birthday, you will remember to show up to court next time."

"I'd remember, man. But this is my birthday."

"There is nothing I can do about it, Curtis. I have to go wake up everybody else. Please go downstairs, get your laundry, and put your clothes away." As I left Curtis's room I thought about throwing him a surprise party, but I knew I could not afford it, and besides my boss would not like the idea. She did not like anything that was different than the daily schedule unless it was her idea. Besides, the judge was trying to teach Curtis a lesson, and I was not about to argue with a judge's orders when it sounds like she was trying to teach Curtis a specific lesson. Besides, even if I had disagreed with the judge's intent, disobeying a judge's orders or the intent of her orders was a quick way to find yourself unemployed or worse.

Breakfast and the chores went normally. When Mike turned on the TV, Curtis was still moping around. Mike was looking for the local college football game. I did not really care for football, but since most of the youths wanted to see the game, I was not going to raise an objection. I just took my newspaper, asked who wanted the sports section, dropped it on the coffee table, and stood back to watch the feeding frenzy. Yup, I still had all ten fingers. I knew that the rest of the morning would be spent watching the game.

Some of the kids soon tired of watching sports and took a board game into the kitchen. I followed them to keep an eye on them and to listen to what they were talking about. This was one way I could make sure that the conversation was appropriate. It also gave me a chance to learn more about each individual kid. This information could be useful during one-on-one counseling sessions. If I could learn what interested a kid, I could find alternative programs that might keep kids busy and out of trouble once they were released.

Lunchtime arrived when the morning game was over. The boys helped set up and clean up. Mike and I arranged a field trip out to a local basketball court. We were required to give each youth the "opportunity" for one hour of physical exertion. Our boss had made it clear that if the youths were acting up, they could have the "opportunity" to physically exert themselves by doing push-ups and sit-ups quietly in their rooms. However, since the youths were behaving themselves today, Mike and I agreed to take them out of the house. Besides, we were also tired of only looking at the four walls of the TV room.

Mike would not tell the kids about our trip until the last minute. We turned off the phone, so that the youths could not call their friends and tell them where we were going. Everybody had a good idea that we were about to leave and so the energy level in the living room was slowly rising. The last clue the kids needed was when I took the basketballs out of the coat closet, and shut off the TV. I did not even have to announce that we were leaving as all of the youths got up and ran upstairs to change into sports clothes. This was what everyone wanted on a warm dry fall day.

When everybody came back to the front door, I took a head count and we all left as a group. We all climbed into the van. Mike drove and I sat in the passenger's chair, half turned to keep an eye on our charges. Mike turned on the radio, and the focus of attention turned to the rap music. Some of the youths started to sing along. Mike would jokingly ask them what they had done with the money he had given them.

"What money?" the kids asked as a chorus.

"The money I gave you for singing lessons," Mike responded. Many of our charges either chuckled at themselves, or put on an act as if they were truly insulted. We would all get a laugh out of it, and then the attention would once again go back to the radio and the off-key choirs of detainees.

We arrived at a local schoolyard and made sure it was empty. Had anyone else been there, we would have needed to find another place to play. Mike pulled the van up, bouncing along the curb, and everyone piled out. Mike looked forward to these games. I knew that this was his opportunity to show the kids his mettle on their terms. I looked to the games as a chance to get a little exercise, and show the youths that I did not take myself so seriously that I would not embarrass myself in front of them. I knew that I could not play that well, but everyone knew that I would play as hard and as long I could.

Some of our charges did not want to play basketball. They would go off to the side and sit on the grass. They would talk about why they were in jail, and how they were not going to be caught the next time. These were usually the youths who came from better homes or could not play very well. We would try to keep them from talking about committing future crimes, but we all knew that our efforts were pointless. We would be seeing them over and over, but almost always for minor stuff.

I would play in a game or two, and then I could sit back, watch, and monitor the conversations of those who were not playing. It concerned me that some of the older youths would try to convince the younger inmates that they knew ways to do crimes and not get caught. I would every once in a while remind these younger clients that the advice was coming from someone who was serving two weeks for taking a car. He was caught and now would have to pay for the damages he caused. I never mentioned that I knew he would be back in three months for refusing to pay that money, but the point had been made. The kid shut his mouth.

I sat back and watched Mike play against Curtis. They were captains of opposing teams. It was pleasure to watch these two as they made it clear to each other that it was more a game of one-on-one than five-on-five. While eight others danced around the court, Mike and Curtis were clearly paired off against each other and looking for ways to "one up" each other. If I had not known better, I might have thought they were two friends playing out a weekend grudge match.

As the game continued, I noticed how most of the trees had lost their leaves and the air was starting have a slight bite. This was a wonderful fall day. I could watch nine of the kids play ball, and the other three were sitting in clear view. If I had not known who these youths were, this would have almost looked like a club outing. Every once in a while a youth would say something about a bad shot that showed I was not supervising a church youth group, but other than that, it was a calm outing.

Mike would continue to play until he was sure that everyone was too tired to continue. When only three other kids were willing to play a fifth game, Mike announced that it was time to return to the facility. The ride back was very similar to the ride out, only most of the kids were much quieter and badly needed to shower.

Arriving back at the house, we let the kids in two at a time. Each youth had to be patted down to verify they were not trying to bring contraband into the facility. The kids made it clear that they objected to this part of an outing, and we made it clear that it was going to happen regardless of their objections and how badly they smelled.

After everyone was in, Mike and I took care of the office details of reporting on the outing. While other kids collapsed onto the living room couch, Mike ordered three of the boys at a time to go upstairs and take a shower. The answering machine was blinking. I pressed the play button only to hear Mike's wife's voice shatter the calm of the afternoon. "Dear, the baby has a fever and has started to throw up again. I've taken her to the hospital; please meet me here when you get off." Mike's expression changed like lightning. The look of terror on his face was clear. I looked at the clock and made an executive decision.

"Mike! Go! Log out as if it is your time to leave. I can handle this group for half an hour until Steve gets here."

"Are you sure?" Mike asked, grabbing his coat.

"Drive carefully!" I responded.

With that, Mike logged out and was out the door. I explained to the youths what had happened. I made it clear that this was not the time to cause any problems. The look on Curtis's face showed his concern. He met the baby when Mike had brought her in the week before. Mike had even let Curtis hold the baby, but only with close supervision of Mike's wife. I walked past him and said softly, "She'll be O.K. She comes from a strong family."

As soon as I sat down, there was a knock at the door. Steve was early. "Where is Mike?" he asked. I explained what had happened and suddenly realized that in the rush of the moment, Mike had forgotten to leave not only his set of door keys, but also the van keys. "I hope you were not looking forward to going anywhere tonight, Steve." We both chuckled. Steve made a few calls and got a hold of Mike at the hospital. They made plans for Mike to bring the keys back later that night. I went into the living room and told a freshly showered Curtis that the baby only had a minor infection and that she would be fine. Curtis tried to look like he did not care, but I knew that he was actually relieved. I chuckled to myself, and went back to the office to share this news with Steve.

When three o'clock hit, I ordered the youths upstairs for quiet time. A few youths would grab a book to read, while others asked if they could take a shower. If the boss had been there, we would have said no, but it was the weekend. One good whiff, and they were not only told they could, but ordered to take a hot shower, since they had not done so when given the opportunity earlier. Steve and I took this opportunity to talk with different kids one-on-one. Technically, we were supposed to let them rest or reflect, but this was the only time that Steve and I had to work with the kids one-on-one, when they were not in trouble.

Curtis was again in his room sitting on the bed. I knocked and walked in. Curtis looked up to acknowledge my presence and then went back to looking out the window. "Is this the first time you have been in detention during your birthday?"

"Nah, I also was in detention during my thirteenth birthday."

"Where were you?" I asked, knowing that there were a large number of different detention locations all over the state.

"I was at Elk Glen, but then I got a day pass to go home with my mother," Curtis responded.

Elk Glen was a long-term juvenile detention facility run by the state. All of the youths there were serving sentences of over thirty days in length and were officially in state custody. "What did you do to get sent there?" I asked.

"Nothing..." He paused for a moment and added, "I got caught beating a kid up at school...who was from another 'hood'."

Having only visited Elk Glen briefly, I was curious as to what Curtis thought about life there.

"It's O.K., I guess. They've got more to do there. They have their own basketball courts, they let us play Nintendo whenever we want, and the food is better," Curtis commented.

I chuckled to myself as I had heard this myth before. Kids always talk up the places they have been before, and complain about the places where they currently are. I knew that next month Curtis would probably be complaining about where he was then and bragging about what things were like here. I guess these kids hope we might be convinced to give them what they want, but it has not worked yet.

Curtis continued, "They have more programs, the school is better, but you need to watch your step."

"Why?" I asked, trying to lead him on.

"They got people from all over there. One wrong move and . . . POW, you on the ground. There are a lot more places where the staff cannot watch you all the time. All it takes is for you to go someplace where it's just you and some other dude from another hood, and if no one is watching, you had better know how to take care of yourself. That's why you need to know who your homies really are, and learn to stay with them."

After a while, I got up and spoke with some of the other youths. My rounds were interrupted by a knock at the door. I went downstairs and found Scott waiting at the door. I let him in and threw the keys at him. "So you are my relief tonight," I commented. I brought him up to date on the day's events, told him about Mike, the keys, and logged out. As I left the facility I asked myself, "Why can't these kids be like this every day?"

ADDITIONAL INFORMATION

Policies and Realities

Your first day on the job you will most likely be handed the program's or facility's policy manual. This could be anything from a few pages to a bound volume. Regardless of its size, read it carefully and remember as much as possible. These will be the rules which will regulate your behavior, your approach, your schedule and your energies. These policies were created by your supervisor and those above him or her. These policies are there to protect the agency, the youths and you. However, following policies can be very difficult in real life situations. As you read the policies remember that you need to be personally comfortable following them.

The easiest situation to work in is one where you can wholeheartedly adopt the policies and expectations of the program in which you are working. This means that you feel morally and professionally comfortable with what is being asked of you. This is the best situation, as it will create the least amount of conflict between you, your supervisors and the program. This type of situation makes it more difficult for youths to take advantage of differences among the staff. However, this is an ideal, and the possibility of finding a program which matches your personality and has an opening right when you are looking for a job is rather low.

The most likely reality is that you will have to adapt to the program in which you are working. This will mean that at first you will have to bend your personality to the policies and expectations of the program as far as you can. In time, by watching other staff and your supervisors you will learn how far the program is willing to bend in order to work with the personality of the staff and the youths currently using the program. The problem with adapting and bending policies is that you expose yourself to risks if anything goes wrong in the program. If a youth gets injured under your care and you were not following policy or protocol you could be held personally responsible, terminated and/or incur great legal expense.

Please remember, eventually all things that are forced to bend too far break. If the policies, expectations or program of your employer will not work with your personality, leave! You do nobody any favors by staying employed at an agency with a different approach than you are willing to take. At best you will earn a few months' salary, be miserable and a get a poor recommendation. At worse you will be the staff member that weakens a program. Youths will start with, "But, so-and-so lets us do it." The clients will use your unwillingness to follow the rules as license for them to do the same. There is nothing wrong with not taking the first job handed to you, or leaving after reading a policy manual that will not work for you. In the long run it will make both you and your potential employers much happier.

If you have a difficult time deciding if you can adopt or adapt to your new employer's expectations, program and policies, then watch others. Watch how your supervisor interacts with the other staff and the youths. Would you be comfortable taking orders from them, given their interpretation of these rules? Watch the staff to learn if they accept the rules as their own, or do they bend them and how far. Are the staff taking on undue liability because they feel the policies don't work? Watch how the youths behave. Do the youths know what is expected of them and how much they can get away with, or are they constantly testing the limits? A constant testing of limits is a good sign that different staff members let the youths get away with more or less unacceptable behaviors. It is these differences which can create the peaceful afternoon described in this chapter or hours of conflict and strife. The enforcing of rules which staff are not comfortable following can create the risks described in the next chapter.

MAJOR POINTS

1) Policies are there for a reason. They are written by elected officials, judges, state agencies, program directors and supervisors, within the context of the law. When interpreting them try to remember the reason for which they were written.

2) Always look to those with more experience for guidance. Do not be afraid to ask for, or receive, advice!

3) Know yourself. Are your personality, social philosophy and moral principles consistent with the policies of the program by which you are employed? If the answer is no, then you need to find employment elsewhere!

CLASS ACTIVITIES

1) Go to a local youth agency and read its policy manual. Talk to the staff about these policies. Does the staff remember the policies and follow them? Watch how the staff handles difficult situations. Are the staff doing what they told you they did? If they do not follow a policy, is there a clear reason why? Take what you observe and participate in a full class discussion of each student's observations.

2) In a group of four students, select a local agency and a daily situation that the agency might face. As a group, create a one-page policy for staff members to follow in this situation. Remember to write your policies based on liability, safety and resource issues. Then take your policy and trade it with another group. Evaluate the policy you have been given. Does it deal with the situation described? Could you follow this policy if you were the employee?

Chapter 8
Why Riot?

QUESTIONS TO THINK ABOUT AS YOU READ
1) How well or poorly do you deal with changes in your daily routine?
2) What methods do you use to adapt to these changes? Are these methods different if the change is caused by others?
3) How do these coping methods affect others around you?

READING

Sundays could be just like Saturdays. They could be laid back, calm, and enjoyable. They could also be hectic, chaotic, and busy. I never knew what to expect when I left for work. I knew that the traffic was going to be very interesting.

The freeway was still under construction. Most drivers had still not figured out that the best way to keep moving was to get into one lane and stay there. The other drivers kept jumping from the one side of the freeway to the other, but got no further ahead. After five minutes of being upset with the others on the road, I realized that this frustration was getting me no satisfaction. I needed to just sit back and listen to the radio.

When I finally did arrive at work, I was five minutes late. The person I was scheduled to replace was already climbing the walls. As soon as I knocked on the door, it was open, the keys were in my hand, and he was gone. I only saw the blur of his face, and it looked like he had had a "fun" shift.

I walked into the office directly and found David sitting at the desk. David was an "on-call" employee, who came in whenever one of the regular team could not make it in or suddenly quit. "Is Mike still dealing with the baby?" I asked.

"I guess so. I think you had better read the log," David responded.

I read that last night two of the youths were caught upstairs without permission. Scott had gone upstairs to investigate and found them smoking. He found the cigarettes, but did not find matches or a lighter. Suddenly the smoke alarm went off. While Steve was making sure that everyone had left the building safely, Scott found that someone had put a single staple in both sides of an electrical socket. The staple had gotten red hot and was melting the plastic cover. Scott had grabbed a towel and pulled the red-hot clip out, mildly burning himself in the process.

When the fire department came they inspected the house and praised Scott for his quick thinking. They cared for his "wounds," and shut off the fire alarm, returning the program to "normal." Scott then called the boss to inform her of the incident, and to try to get permission to return our two arsonists to the main detention unit.

The boss had asked him why the two boys were upstairs unsupervised in the first place. When Scott could not explain why they were upstairs unsupervised to her satisfaction, she questioned his ability to do his job. Scott pointed out that he had kept the house from catching fire, and that he had followed proper procedure in dealing with the incident. He was surprised when the boss hung up on him abruptly. He was even more surprised when he got a phone call an hour later telling him that he was fired, and that he was supposed to leave the facility when his replacement came in thirty minutes. Scott had asked why he should have to stay and wait for a replacement. When the boss could not give him a reasonable response, Scott explained that he would stay at the facility, if only to prove himself better and more professional than our supervisor. He then hung up the phone and documented this entire transaction in the facility log, where all of the staff could read his account of events.

I was taken aback. Scott had been one of our better counselors. The kids responded well to him and worked well with him. He had come from a similar background as many of our clients; then he converted to Islam and had cleaned up his act over five years ago. He was very careful not to push his religion on the kids, but if they asked, he was happy to share. I was going to be sorry to see him leave. It also meant that I would probably have to stay and work a second shift, as Scott was supposed to be my replacement tonight.

Then I noticed the client board. The entire program of activities had been shut down by order of the boss and one of the two who started the fire was still here. She felt that if a small group of youths had acted out, we should punish the whole group. That way, she believed, the older youths would keep the younger ones from starting trouble. Those of the staff with military experience tried to explain to her that this system would only work if there were illegal threats of violent intimidation by the larger and older kids toward the younger ones. She did not believe us. A shut down program could mean an easy day, or a pain.

After expressing my anger to David over the Scott situation, he recommended that I continue to read the log. There had been an escape. One of the two who had been caught smoking was last seen at lights out, and an hour later he was gone. Procedures were followed, but his property had still to be taken into storage (my job included controlling the properties of escapees). I was informed that the youths were not happy about the room restriction, and they had learned from the night shift that it was not our idea. "By the way, I moved the twit who started the fire downstairs to keep him away from the other kids. I did not want him to get his face kicked in while I was using the restroom. And now for your pleasure, Josh, there is a group of boys on the stairs who would like to discuss the issue with you."

"Thanks," I grumbled as I left the office door. "Why do I get to deal with it?"

"Because you are the senior staff on duty," he chirped.

Sitting on the stairs were six boys of mixed ages. It was still eight in the morning so they were not yet completely awake. Two were dressed. Two were in pajamas. The final two sat there only in their boxer shorts. I was not impressed.

"O.K., what is this about?"

"Why do we have to stay in our rooms all day, when it was that white boy upstairs who started the fire?"

I had to think about my answer. These boys could tell when I was lying. These kids practiced telling lies to each other all day. They knew how to watch somebody's body and face to see if they were lying or not. Since I was no expert at lying, the only option left to me was to tell the truth. Even here I had to be careful because these kids could also recognize hypocrisy, and would point it out if they thought it was to their advantage. I could re-explain our policy on group discipline, but this would accomplish nothing. "Now you know the way this program works," I tried to start.

"Look man, if you forget about shutting the program down and let us watch TV, we won't tell anyone."

"Right," I responded sarcastically. "The minute I leave, and someone else tries to enforce the boss's orders, you are going to sit there and say '. . . but Josh let us do it.'" I paused, "I wish I did not have to do this, but it is the boss's orders and we will make sure they are enforced. Now, remember, you work with me, and we can all get what we want. The boss has ordered that the living room needs to be completely cleaned. This means that all of the books should come off the shelves, the shelves dusted, the books dusted, and returned to the shelves. Now while everyone is cleaning, I'll supervise. I think I can supervise your cleaning while watching a football game or two. Now, you are not to be watching the game, you are to clean every ounce of dust off the furniture and the shelves. I even want the chairs turned upside-down and cleaned. The fact that the TV is located in the living room is purely coincidental. Once the chores are done, everyone will go to their rooms and stay there, except for meals. Any questions?"

The older boys looked at me, grinned, and then started to go to their rooms. The younger boys looked like they were going to object, and then decided that it was not worth their time. I probably gave these boys too much, but I was left in the impossible position of trying to control 11 angry adolescents who were being punished for the actions of one of them. This situation had to be carefully controlled; otherwise, it could easily get out of hand. Walking into the office, I looked up and asked David, "Do you think I went too far?"

"No. I think you responded correctly. I don't feel like putting down a riot and having the supervisor asking questions about my 'counseling abilities,'" David responded with clear sarcasm in his voice.

"I don't like it when she puts us in a difficult situation, and then expects us to solve the problem. If you then call her about it, and ask for her assistance, you know she will hit the roof for interrupting her evening. I just don't want to deal with it. How much about Scott do the kids know?"

"They know the whole thing. They are not happy about it, and a few even asked what they could do to help him."

"Great, I hope that they are not going to take it out on us."

"It's been taken care of, so you don't have to worry. By the way, Mike is at home with the baby today. He wanted to spend the day with his family after yesterday's scare."

"That makes sense," I commented. "I have to remember to ask him how the fishing went, when I see him tomorrow." It was an inside joke that whenever Mike told the boss he was taking a day off for the family, he was usually fishing. Sometimes he actually took one of his children with him, but we all knew that he liked to spend his quiet time sitting with his eyes closed, fishing rod in hand, by the side of any of the local lakes.

After reading all of the logs and catching up with my morning paperwork, I went into the kitchen to set up breakfast, only to find that the food had not yet arrived. When I asked, I was informed that the central kitchen was running about two hours behind schedule. This meant that breakfast would not arrive until 0830. I grumbled, "Are there any other disasters you have not told me about that I'm going to have to deal with today?"

"Well, before you arrived the president called, and asked for your advice on how to deal with the economy and Congress."

"Oh good, a simple problem to deal with," I responded, sitting at my desk looking over the paperwork on the office wall.

When I was done rereading the cartoons that had been on the wall for as long as I had worked here, I started to read the Sunday paper I had brought with me. My reading was interrupted by a knock on the door, announcing the arrival of breakfast. David jumped up to go get it. I looked at the clock and realized that it was time to waken everybody upstairs.

I went to wake everyone up and found that most everybody was awake and had already heard about my earlier discussions. No one was thrilled with the outcome, but nobody wanted to push their luck and have me not "watch a football game," which I really did not want to see in the first place. Breakfast was eaten in an uneasy silence. The chores and Sunday deep cleaning were started. While everyone tried to get all of the dirt out of the sofas, I was watching the local team get destroyed on the field. It was clear that this game was going to be a blow out by the start of the second quarter. Heck, we knew that this game was going to be a blow out after the second game of the season. This was going to be just another poor showing for our hometown teams. Some of the kids asked me to change it to the Philadelphia game, but I reminded them that they were cleaning, and I was supervising. When I finally officially recognized that the chores were done, and everyone was just sitting around and watching, I told everybody to grab a book if they wanted it, and to go to their rooms. I had to deal with the usual complaining, but in time it was clear that I was going to win this debate for now.

". . . But it's the Lord's Day, we need to have a bible study," one of the older kids mumbled.

I could not believe that these kids were still using the old "I've found religion" ploy. All I could do to keep from laughing was to shake my head and say, "You did not need bible study last week, when you wanted to go play basketball."

"We are trying to reform ourselves," came an answer from one of the youths toward the top of the stairs. It was clear that he was grasping for any straw available.

"Ken, I will believe that you have reformed yourself when you can go for one year without stealing anything. Until then, we will keep a room for you here with your name on it."

"Oh, man. You get in a little bit of trouble, and you have to put up with his mouth," Ken responded as he started to move to his room. After checking to make sure that everybody was where they were supposed to be, I made my rounds and talked with a few of the youths to see if I could make any progress with them. It was clear that many of the kids did not want to discuss anything, other than getting out of their rooms, and watching the tube. Even Curtis was sitting in his room not wanting to talk. So I left him with the sports section and went to go get the rest of the paper. David and I sat in the upstairs hallway to try to keep the pranks to a minimum, and both of us read. I had my paper and David read his philosophy book. This was going to be a long boring morning.

When lunch came, everybody was still upset, or just waking up from a nap. I knew that those who had been napping would have a problem getting to sleep later tonight, but there was not much I could do about it. When lunch was over, some kids grumbled about having to clean up after the meal. Most of them got up after the meal, leaving their plates where they were, and went upstairs to their rooms. This was the youths' way of telling us that they were getting testy about having to stay in their rooms any longer. I realized that I could keep the lid on it for a bit longer, but that sooner or later I might have to bend the boss's orders a little bit more, or else there was going to be more difficulty. But how far could I bend it, before I was just ignoring the order?

David and I discussed how we were going to solve the looming confrontation. I suggested that we leave the kitchen a mess and have the kids clean it before dinner. David suggested that we clean up the mess ourselves. After talking about options for five minutes, I decided that I would rather not wait until the kids chose to confront us, but rather we would deal with this here and now.

David called down all the kids from upstairs for a house meeting. The meeting would run according to a well set pattern. I would state what the problem was, the kids would raise their objections, and then we would come to an official solution, which I would log. We would also agree on how we could actually circumvent the approaching confrontation.

Curtis took the lead among the guys and spoke for the group. If Curtis had not spoken up, someone else like Ken would have. Curtis objected to the fact that he was being punished for what someone else did. I noticed that the remaining kid who started all of this trouble was keeping quiet in the corner, hoping not to be noticed. I explained that the program was set up based on group behavior. "When one member of the group makes a mess, everybody has to clean it up. If you don't like cleaning up messes, try to keep your homies from causing trouble."

"He's not my homie," Curtis said in a gruff voice.

"That fine," I said, "but unfortunately you are in detention together, and so you have to obey the rules set up for this detention program together."

I knew that Curtis could start by going into his story about not yet being convicted, but he knew that it would get him nowhere, so we instead looked for a middle ground. It was finally agreed that everybody would clean up from lunch, and that I would call down everyone for dinner at 1630, when the post-game shows would be on. They could wait in the living room for dinner, and I would "accidentally" leave it on so that they could find out how their teams did. This seemed an acceptable solution. So while they cleaned up the kitchen, I logged that we had the problem, followed by a house meeting. "The meeting ended with the kids cleaning up the kitchen," I logged. I did not like the feeling that I was lying, but I had been placed in an impossible predicament, and I had found a solution to both my and the kids' problems. Even David was happy with the solution.

When four o'clock came, I waited for the replacement to show up. I knew that there was a fifty-fifty chance I would still be here in eight hours. Fifteen minutes later, I still had no replacement. I called up my supervisor and asked if I was going to be relieved. I knew that she was not going to be in a good mood, but I knew that if I took the second shift without conferring with her, she would also have a snit. As I had suspected, she was gruff with me, but when I suggested that I could stay the extra shift, she started to calm down. She also made it clear that my life would be much easier if I agreed to take the extra shift on Thursday. I agreed, if only to find a way to hang up the phone quickly. Before she let me go, she asked if the program was still shut down. "Yes, it is," I responded. She was pleased that the problems had been solved without her. As I put the phone down, I was relieved that I was not going to need to explain to her that I was about to let everyone downstairs for setting up dinner.

"David, weren't you supposed to leave two hours ago?" I asked.

"I am also working a double shift today."

I called down all the kids to "help prepare for dinner." I explained to everybody that David and I were going to have to be here for another eight hours each, and that it would be to everybody's advantage not to cause either of us any grief. Some of these clients suggested that they had no sympathy for us, as we were here by choice and we could go home at the end of the day. A quick glare from David or me put a quick end to any of these vocal objections.

After dinner was cleaned up, I suggested that they take some games up to their rooms. I told them that since the fire alarm went off at 1900 hours last night, I would turn on the TV for everyone at 1900 hours. That is, if there were no further problems. The kids looked at each other and agreed that this was a fair solution or at least the best they were going to get from me tonight. The kids grabbed a few games and went up to their room. It was humorous to watch a game board in the middle of the hall, being played by two people in different rooms. On one board there were three people playing one game. I was glad that they were doing quiet activities, without causing any problems.

When 1900 came, everybody came downstairs, the TV and pay phone were turned on, and people lined up for quarters so they could use the pay phone. Once the phone's pecking order was determined, the house was calm. I called Curtis into the office and talked with him about how he became a responsible group leader. Curtis just shrugged it off again, and asked if he could go out to watch TV. I knew that he really did not want to talk right now, so I let him return to the living room. At 2100 hours, I sent everybody to their rooms, and by 2200 hours David's replacement came into a quiet calm house. By midnight, I was relieved and on my way home for six hours of sleep. I always hated having a double shift, followed by an hour drive home, five to six hours of sleep, an hour drive back, and then one more shift. I was so glad when my one-day weekend arrived!

ADDITIONAL INFORMATION
Crisis Management

The art of crisis management requires the ability to keep the illusion of control. You may not personally feel in control of the situation, but the clients must believe that you are. Once the illusion is lost, it becomes almost impossible to take control without drastic changes to the situation. So once you realize you are in a crisis situation, take controlled steps to keep the illusion that you are in control and know what you are doing.

The situation described in this chapter is neither a worst- or best-case scenario. The clients are still in control of their emotions and are looking for a solution to what they see as an unfair punishment. If this was a facility where youths could be locked into rooms where they could only do minimal damage, then a negotiated settlement would not have been necessary. Also, both of the staff members would need to be comfortable with the orders, or at least able to make the youths believe they were comfortable with the orders they had received, in order to enforce them properly.

In this situation, you have a facility where the youths cannot be physically controlled against their will and you have to enforce orders which are going to be unpopular. In addition, the staff as described in the text are both uncomfortable with the orders, and neither would or could use the perception of physical intimidation to get what they want. So a negotiated settlement is necessary.

What is not negotiable is the overall order from the supervisor that all extra program activities are canceled. The youths know that this order has been given, and if you refuse to carry it out, that the youths have potential "blackmail" material to use against you. By threatening to tell your supervisor what you did not do, they can coerce you into bending the rules more. Further, since what you are supposed to be teaching is a respect for authority, directly disobeying a known order will not be setting an appropriate example. So staff must look for ways that they can follow orders and adapt it to the reality of the situation.

This solution is one that only worked because of the situation. If the youths were not willing to negotiate, or were already out of control, then a negotiated settlement would not have solved the problem. Ironically, the solution comes from the other difficult order from the supervisor that the TV room should be cleaned from top to bottom. This gives the staff the opportunity to adapt both orders to their personalities, while giving the youths a motivation to continue to follow the staff's directions.

Self-control vs. Group control

As stated before, you must control yourself before you can control others. In the story two young adults are left to control eleven angry youths. In any challenging event, the first thing you must do is take a deep breath. Do not allow yourself to hyperventilate, but take deep controlled breaths that give you time to think before you act. Keep your voice low, deep, and controlled. A high-pitched voice should only be used with small children and during play periods. When your authority is being questioned, you must show you are in control of your speech. Stay aware of your body language. Keep your arms to your side or in front of your chest. Make sure your hands and arms are available for defense, without being threatening to others. Keep your eyes focused on the others around you. Do not look at the ground, or away from the potential threats, but rather look at these people directly. Finally, keep your shoulders back and loose, so you look confident and in control. However, your body control is only one part of self-control.

In a difficult situation, you must also keep your mental sense of self. If you do not believe that you can control the situation, others will see it. You must have faith in your own ability to weather any storm. Part of this ability requires you to put your doubts into the back of your mind, and present an act to those with whom you are working. A well performed act of confidence can make others follow you, even if they have their own concerns or issues.

In order to make you act convincing, you will need to practice putting yourself into stressful situations where you can make mistakes safely. While you are still in school, volunteer in a number of youth programs. Make sure you volunteer to lead a few programs and activities. If you are not comfortable speaking publicly, or in confrontations, join a debate club or practice giving public presentations. Many people who may appear confident in public situations are just practiced. If you ask them, they may honestly say that they are not comfortable, but that they have practiced their act of confidence. A strong act of confidence is a great tool to possess in any difficult situation.

Group vs. Individual Responsibility

This chapter raises the issue of whether to hold a group or an individual responsible when a behavior or event is not acceptable. With group punishment, the worker does not need to find out who is individually responsible for the events in question. It is appropriate where an event has occurred wherein most of the clients, class or youths have played some role in the incident or when due to group safety you need to make a quick decision. The problem with punishing the whole group is that those who were not involved in causing the problems will also be punished. It is completely inappropriate to use group punishment to try to get the clients to regulate their own behavior, as this will require the larger, more powerful youths to intimidate the smaller ones through the use of violence. Not only does this create a dangerous environment, but it also assumes that the larger youths can and will intimidate others into better behavior.

Individual punishment is ideal. When you can figure out who is responsible and hold them accountable, then you are not also punishing those clients who acted appropriately. However, it is not always possible to discover who is responsible for causing the events you are investigating. Also, when you have some youths who are being punished and others who are not, this will take extra time and manpower to supervise both groups. Besides, it is not unusual for one person to act out based on the suggestion of another.

Learning

When you graduate from college, you will be trained in the newest and most up-to-date approaches. You will also have been taught why some older approaches are being abandoned or improved. Armed with this knowledge, you walk into your first job, only to discover that your supervisors or coworkers still favor some of these older approaches. How will you respond to this conflict of training versus reality?

The supervisor in this book has been created to demonstrate difficult situations in which you might find yourself, and is not meant to be a model for how supervisors actually perform. Supervisors today are usually out of school for many years, but that does not mean that they have abandoned training. Many supervisors attend regular workshops, night classes or university programs to keep their training current. Many of these supervisors also have a clear understanding that what works in the laboratory or under controlled tests, may not work for them or their employees in the real world. Good supervisors realize that different employees will use different approaches. They will watch you not just to criticize, but to help you refine your approaches to make you more compatible with the program and the youths with whom you are working. Always remember, watch your supervisor for what you can learn from them.

Your coworkers were there before. They know what it is like to be in a new situation and to feel unsure of yourself. They also know that youths will give you many severe tests during your first months in a program. Look to your coworkers for guidance. In my first real shift in juvenile detention I was assigned to work with a real Mike (see chapter 1). He never attended college, but he did serve in the military as a police officer. He was shorter and smaller than I was, but he taught me the most about how to survive in this reality. He had grown up on the streets, lived his life like most of the youths with whom we worked, and learned firsthand what it takes to turn a life around. He taught me how to carry myself and act with authority, even though most of the youths were taller than both of us. The point is to look to all of your coworkers for guidance, and for what they can teach you, no matter what their background and training.

While much of what the youths may tell a new employee will get you in trouble, remember that they might also be trying to help you. These youths most likely have known each other for a long time. They know what makes the other people angry or happy. As youths learn to trust you, you will be able to ask them for information about other youths with whom you are working. They might also tell you when you are doing things that could get you in trouble with other youths (like the dangers of wearing red sweaters with blue pants, as these are conflicting gang signs). Listen to what the youths have to tell you; the lesson may be worth your time.

One of these lessons is clearly demonstrated in this past chapter. This is the need for the illusion of control. In the situation described, there are two staff members working with eleven or twelve youths with the potential for violence.

It is important to listen to them and watch for any signs that you might be losing control of the situation. It is better to have a confrontation in a meeting rather than risk a fight over which you have no control. In order to make the meeting work, you need to have the illusion that you are in complete control of them and yourself. These youths know that there are twelve of them and they could easily overpower two staff members in a fight, but by the staff keeping the illusion that they are in control, it keeps the youths from taking the initiative and threatening everyone's safety. In all situations, it is your responsibility to watch for variables that might threaten your control and take appropriate steps to avoid that possibility.

The appropriate steps will be dictated by the constantly changing attitudes of the various youths with whom you are working and your own personality. As a youth worker you need to constantly be aware of the social environment in which you are working. Are they becoming agitated, or are they calming down? You then need to measure any input you add into the situation. Be aware of how this input will be received by the youths with whom you are working. Will your response make the situations worse or bring things better under control?

A major factor in how your responses will be received will depend on your physical appearance. A six-foot-seven inch, 250-pound male will be able to use approaches that a 5-foot, 120-pound female could not, only because his size is more intimidating. The smaller female will need to have better control of her body language and be able to appear in control and prepared for anything. Remember that a well-controlled properly postured short woman can have greater physical presence than a large male with bad posture and frayed nerves. Be aware of how you will be perceived by the youths and learn ways to use this perception to your advantage in controlling any situation.

MAJOR POINTS

1) In life, you will have to find comfortable ways to deal with conflicts. If you are using methods you are not comfortable with, youths will use your discomfort to take advantage of you and the situation.

2) If you are not comfortable with your employer's methods of dealing with conflict, you will need to adapt to their methods. If you cannot adapt to your supervisor, and your supervisor refuses to work with your personality, than you need to find employment elsewhere. You are doing nobody any favors by staying in an employment situation where both you and your employer will not be satisfied.

CLASS ACTIVITIES

1) Go back to the local youth agency and volunteer for at least an afternoon. Watch the different power relations between the director, staff, volunteers and the youth. Return to your class and discuss what you observed. What methods would you be comfortable using? What methods could you adapt to your personality? Compare the physical size and personal presence of the various people you observed. What methods would not work for you at all?

2) Write a one-page paper about a disagreement you had with a supervisor, instructor or professor. Explain how you and the other person dealt with the conflict. Were you satisfied with the outcome of the situation? How might you have better handled the situation?

Chapter 9
An Incomplete Sentence

QUESTIONS TO THINK ABOUT AS YOU READ
1) How well do you adapt to physical and/or psychological stress?
2) How often do court cases actually go to trial? Who does this benefit?
3) Can juvenile courts make the punishment fit the crime? Should they?

READING

Most people would call today Monday. For me it is Wednesday. I might not have noticed the difference, except for the increased traffic on the freeway. This was the first day of work for most of these people, when it came to dealing with the road construction in the middle lanes. I had already figured out how best to dodge the construction islands; unfortunately, the Monday to Friday commuters did not have a clue. I was not going to be late to work; I had planned for this. The part I hated was sitting and waiting for everyone else to learn the new game.

Upon arriving at work, I performed my morning greetings to my coworker, who had arrived four hours early. Sarah was picking up a few extra hours herself. We got straight down to the business of splitting of the daily duties. The calendar showed that today Ken was supposed to be at court in the afternoon for sentencing. Sarah and I had to figure out which of us would take him to court, and who would have to stay here and watch the rest of the kids. The calendar also showed that two other kids were supposed to be released today.

"You got to go to court the last time. Now it's my turn," Sarah started.

"I went the last time, because I worked a double shift the day before. Again yesterday, I worked two day shifts in a row. I've only had five hours of sleep again last night and I would really prefer to take Ken to court."

"If I let you take him to court, will you get me a cola?" Sarah asked.

"Can you pay for it? I am a little tight right now," I answered.

"How can you be tight for money, when you are the one working all these extra shifts?"

"I just got married. You do remember that I need the money to move out of my in-laws' house?"

"Funny, I thought that you were going to pay for the move, using your charm and good looks."

"Let's see, my charm and good looks will get me . . . an empty tank of gas in my van and bus ride to nowhere," I jabbed back.

This solved the problem of today's scheduling. With this, we began the daily schedule. It was clear that the kids were going to have a typical day. They got up on time, except for two who had to be woken up five times each. I finally got them to move when I threatened them with a pot of ice water. I got the kids to finish the chores and get ready for school with thirty minutes to spare. I was already starting to feel the effects of yesterday, but I knew that I needed to finish this shift. It is hard enough to stay awake during the school day when you are fully rested. I have no idea how I managed to stay awake during the classes. I found out later that some of the kids were betting on how long into school it would be before I stared to snore. Fortunately, I won that bet, barely.

Upon returning from school, I was informed that after Ken's hearing, I was supposed to pick up two new kids down from intake. Sarah had everything ready to go, so all I would have to do is bring them here, and someone else would orient the new residents. "They are both repeats," Sarah informed me. I looked at the names, and recognized both of them. They were here on my first days at the home, and were responsible for my "baptism of fire." "I am going to enjoy this. . .I think I'll go schedule a root canal for tomorrow... hold the Novocain."

"Well, you're going to be in a great mood for the rest of the week," Sarah quipped.

I started to catch up on my morning log entrees. Sarah grabbed two of the kids to set up lunch. Halfway through my work, a kid came into the office with a plate of food. I looked up and thanked him for bringing it to me.

"Are you feeling O.K.?" Tim asked. Tim was a twelve-year-old who was serving time for Assault Four from a street fight and minor in possession of alcohol.

"Yeah, I'm fine. I just need to get more sleep tonight," I answered.

"When did you get home last night?"

"I think I got home around 0100 hours and to sleep by 0130. I got up at 0600 hours, so that I could get here on time."

Tim seemed to comprehend, and moved out of the office quickly, rather than testing his luck with a tired staffer. I was left alone to finish my paperwork.

I looked up at the food that was on my plate and between my exhaustion, and the appearance of the food, I lost my appetite. I was going to try to avoid eating this "chicken" casserole, but I knew that was not to be. Sarah came into the office. "I think it would be good for you to eat something, before you go to court," Sarah mothered.

"If this was a weekend shift, Mike and I would remind each other of the golden phrase of institutional food, 'Pizza is delivered!'" I responded.

"You have a choice," Sarah started. "You can put it in your mouth, or I will put it in your EAR."

I grumbled to myself something about her being a coworker and not my mother-in-law. I lifted the fork to my mouth. It actually tasted a little better than it looked, but not much better. I ate five bites before I returned to my paperwork. The volume of the conversation in the kitchen was rising, so Sarah and I went back to our charges to instruct them on cleaning up.

Once the kitchen was cleaned, Sarah turned on the TV and came in to remind me to prepare for taking Ken to court. I grabbed my coat, my organizer, and my current writing project. I did not actually believe that I was going to need my organizer, but I did not want to leave it lying around. My organizer held more than just phone numbers and dates. I also used it to keep track of personal information from the job. This meant everything from which days I had worked extra shifts, to special orders I had received, to kids I had provided counseling to and what we talked about. I might never need this information, but I wanted to have it in case I needed to answer questions about my past actions. Also, this was information that I did not want to share with my coworkers or supervisor, so I kept the book with me.

While Ken and I walked across the parking lot to court, Ken was talking trash about how he was going to be sentenced and then walk free. He was convinced that with time served, he would be walking out after court. I hoped that he was going to be wrong, for the lesson in humility it might teach him, but I knew better than to expect too much. I had seen much more illogical outcomes when I worked as an intern in a different juvenile court, so I was prepared for anything. We walked in, signed in, and sat down. Ken started to work on his "innocent" look and I began to work on my current writing project. Ken just sat there quietly, with bad posture, withdrawn eyes, and sunken shoulders.

We were there for an hour and a half, while I wrote in my book, and Ken was really beginning to look pathetic. Every time I took a good look at him, I just shook my head. It continued like this for a few more minutes until a judge walked by looked at him. "Hi, Ken. Going before my court, again?" Ken got a good look at the judge, and suddenly he began to really look pathetic. I wanted to break out in laughter. I managed to keep it down to a minor chuckle. I noticed that the judge walked into Courtroom Four, and we were supposed to go to Courtroom Three. I could point this out to Ken, but I enjoyed the fact that his cockiness was now subdued.

It was an hour later, when we were finally called into Courtroom Three. Ken's face showed his delighted surprise, as he realized that this courtroom had an on-call judge, who did not know him, his real attitude or his record. This was probably a prosecutor from the adult system who had been called to fill an opening when the regular judge was called to fill an opening in the adult system. What this meant to us was that this young fill-in judge probably had no idea of the depths of Ken's behavioral problems.

Ken moved to sit down next to his court-appointed attorney while I took a seat directly behind him. After a few minutes of paper shuffling, the prosecutor stood up to address the judge. She was a shorter woman, who made her presence known by dressing in a smart business suit and spoke in deep controlled tones. "Your honor, we are here in the case Regal County vs. Ken Davis. Mr. Davis was found guilty at trial of the charge of Taking an Automobile without Permission. Mr. Davis has 3.25 previous points."

The judge interrupted the prosecutor to get her to explain what "previous points" meant. The prosecutor was visibly pleased that this judge had the courage to admit that he did not understand the juvenile court's point system. The prosecutor carefully explained that this was based on five previous similar charges and six other minor charges. When the prosecutor was convinced that the judge understood every conviction on Ken's record, she continued with the standard speech. "The standard range for a youth with this conviction and his record is fifty to ninety days of confinement. Given Mr. Davis's past record and his unwillingness to work with his probation officer, I am requesting that the court impose a sentence at the high end of the range." The judge asked the prosecutor to clarify a few details in her presentation. The prosecutor calmly explained the matters of protocol that were standard for the juvenile court. "In addition, I am asking for an additional 10 hours community service, to be added to Mr. Davis's unfinished community service and an additional six months of community supervision (probation). Finally, I have here receipts from the victim totaling $1200, and he is asking for restitution. I would ask that the court grant this amount, unless the defense attorney would like to have a separate restitution hearing?" the prosecutor asked.

The defense attorney looked up from his files. "Does this $1200 include any repairs that were paid for by insurance?"

"No! The total damage to the victim's vehicle was over $5000. The $1200 only covers his deductibles, and those repairs and losses not covered by insurance. It does not even include payment for time lost by the victim for obtaining estimates and repairs." The prosecutor's voice was firm and clear. She had definitely had enough of this youth's behavior, and did not want him to get away with anything else.

"Your honor," the defense attorney answered, "I do not see the point to having a separate restitution hearing, and we agree to the prosecutor's figures." Everyone in the room breathed a silent sigh of relief, as a restitution hearing could take up to three hours, and usually led to a crime victim feeling twice injured. The victim must justify every expense they are claiming and justify it with two or three professional estimates, which they collected on their own time. A restitution hearing can be very hard for anyone to sit through.

When the prosecutor finished her presentation, the defense attorney rose. "Your honor, I would ask that the court take into consideration the recent behavior of my client. He is currently serving two hours a week of community service, and is looking for employment. He is in a stable relationship with a young lady who is preparing to deliver their first child in a few months. I would ask that for her sake, the court impose a sentence of time served, and impose more community service rather than making my client spend additional time in detention. In detention he will not be able to provide support for his future child." The defense attorney continued for five minutes with his client's plans for the future. I was very pleased with my self-control for not yelling "Bullshit!" during the defense portion of the hearing. I was listening to the same kid being praised who yesterday tried to start a riot because he could not watch a football game.

Now the probation officer rose. Probation officers in juvenile court have expanded duties. They are present at almost all hearings, and must be prepared to make sentencing or release recommendations to the judge. As his probation officer began her presentation, Ken sank visibly into his chair. "Your honor, I have been working with Mr. Ken Davis for the past nine months, since I received his file from my predecessor. During this time he has missed no less than fifty percent of his appointments, and has refused to pay *any* of his past restitution, which now totals $25,530. In addition, he has failed to take any responsibility for his action. The girlfriend to whom the defense attorney referred had to come to my office to get assistance from Mr. Davis, who suddenly left his residence of record, without informing the court. What is more, Mr. Davis has only made plans to find a job; he has made no actual efforts, no resumes, no applications and has contacted no actual employers, to my knowledge. Your honor, given Mr. Davis's poor record of fulfilling his commitments, I request that you acknowledge that the time for leniency is over. This young man needs a clear signal that his poor behavior will no longer be tolerated and that he cannot expect to be treated like a little child any longer."

As his probation officer sat down, I felt relieved that someone was finally acknowledging this young man's destructive potential. This relief was short-lived as the judge gave out his sentence. "Since Mr. Davis is about to be a father, I am prepared to acknowledge that this experience can change him for the better. I therefore order a sentence of ninety days, with all but twenty-five days suspended. In addition, he will be required to serve 45 hours of community service, and shall be required to pay an additional $1200 in restitution to the victim of his crime, in repayment for the damage done to his vehicle. If Mr. Davis appears before this court again for any reason, the full suspended sentence will be imposed."

Ken and I were both counting on our fingers, and both of us came to the quick conclusion that he had already served sixteen days. I watched as Ken whispered this fact into his attorney's ears. His attorney rose and asked the judge that if it is found that he has already served more than twenty-five days, that his client's extra time be used against his community service time. The judge agreed at the rate of one day of detention equal to eight hours of community service. The prosecutor looked like she was about to rise to object to this order, but rather than argue, she just sat back in her chair and shook her head. This meant that Ken would only have to work an additional 29 hours, if he actually did any at all. Ken also knew that these additional community service hours and the 74 suspended jail-time hours could easily be forgotten in paper shuffling and the constant changing of probation counselors. Even with the new computer system, each kid's files were organized by case, not by the child's name. It could be difficult to isolate the exact number of jail days each youth potentially owned. It was a rare kid who had the same probation officer for more than a year, as people left the office, got promoted or went back to school. I did not think it was very likely that Ken would ever serve any more additional time for stealing and destroying someone's car. Ken was very pleased with himself.

I prepared to take Ken back to detention. His probation officer rose and came over to speak with me. "I need to take Ken upstairs and process him out," she said, to my surprise.

"I cannot do that," I responded. "He is currently in detention, my responsibility, and I do not have instructions from the detention placement office to release him to anyone. If I permit him to go with you without a release order from placement, I will be responsible for any trouble he gets into before we discharge him from our program."

"I will fax it over to your facility shortly," she answered.

"I wish that were good enough. Unfortunately the last time I released a kid to his probation officer, I was almost fired for 'not following proper procedure,'" I answered, trying to control my voice.

"You know that if you release him, and just instruct him to come see me, he will walk out your door, and I will not see him until he is arrested again?" she asked.

"Yes, I know," I concede, "but the only way I can release him to you is if the head of placement orders me to release him to you. Because without a paper trail, I will be responsible for any damage done by or to him, until I actually do receive permission and formally sign him out. Now, if you can find her and she will sign an order for me to release him to you, that should work."

"Just a moment, I'll go see if I can find her," the probation officer suggested and disappeared out of the door. In less than a minute she was back with the head of the placement office. "You can release Ken to her," she told me. "I will have two new kids for you to pick up at 6:00 P.M. tonight. One of them you were supposed to pick up now, but he is not ready." I grabbed my things and left the court house knowing that I would be seeing Ken Davis again . . . soon.

I returned to the home and reported everything to my coworkers and logged it. I was relieved to look at the clock and know I could go home. I had just worked 25 of the last 33 hours, and I was ready to go to bed.

ADDITIONAL INFORMATION

Personal Notes

Depending on the competence of your supervisor, the friendliness of your coworkers or the hostility of your clientele, you may find it is desirable to keep a C.Y.A. book. C.Y.A. refers to "Cover Your Assets." This is a log of the events of your work day, including who your coworkers were, what youths you worked with, and what you talked to them about. If a youth was injured on your shift, you will want to record events, any signs of injury you noticed and what you did to treat them. In case of a lawsuit by the youth or his family, they will not only name your employer and your supervisor, but you as well. To be honest, you will never know that you need to keep a C.Y.A. book until after you are in a situation which comes back to haunt you. It is recommended that you always keep a C.Y.A. book, because you never know what a youth, coworker or supervisor might do to you until they are already doing it.

This may sound like you need to be paranoid, but remember that most programs also keep some sort of log. This log will contain when a youth is checked into the program, the activities of the day, who participated, when meals were eaten, any unusual occurrences, and what youths were released or left the program. These logs provide the agency and your supervisor not only with a clear picture of what is occurring, but also protection in case of any legal action.

Youth program employers are very concerned about their legal liability. This concern on their part can affect the environment in which you work. Employers may try to limit their liability by blaming an employee for not following policies. It is up to you to be able to explain how you handled a situation and why this was appropriate, months or even years after the fact.

But what do you need to document, and how will it protect you? This is the "$64,000 question." You never know when a youth, coworker or supervisor may make an allegation or what the allegation might be. Therefore, you need to look for situations that might be used against you in any way. A clear example of this is an extended one-on-one counseling session with no other witnesses. To protect yourself, document when it began and ended, who you were with, what you talked about, who you consulted for advice, and anyone who interrupted. This entry can be as simple as: "10 to 10:30 talked to 'Crts' about family and sister, interrupted by Mike @ 10:20." This simple line gives you the knowledge of the boundaries of any event, what you talked about, and that there was someone who came in the middle who did not see anything wrong. In addition to protecting you against false allegations, this log can also serve to remind you of topics clients have discussed with you, so you can improve your ability to work with that specific youth and their problems.

In the best conditions, you can use your book to remind yourself of the specific needs and problems of the youths with whom you are working. It can remind you of tasks you have left unfinished and those you have completed. In bad situations, it will be there to remind you of what you were doing and why.

MAJOR POINTS

1)   You need to know and observe the stress limits of your own body!

2)   Watch your environment and take steps to protect yourself from those who might wish to make gains by hurting you both financially and physically.

CLASS ACTIVITIES

1)   For two days, keep a day log of the events which occur in your life. Log who you speak to and what conversations take place. After the two days have passed, examine what you wrote to see what events might because you trouble if misused. Were you alone with a professor, a member of the opposite sex or looking at confidential material? What might others assume took place?   Share

your log with a partner in your class. What conclusions might they come to about what took place, and how could that be used against you?

Chapter 10
Gunning for Trouble

QUESTIONS TO THINK ABOUT AS YOU READ

1) When working with youths, are individual or group activities more beneficial? How does the context of these activities affect this answer? What types of activities are most realistic, given the resources of any program?

2) What is your approach to time management? Do you have independent discipline? Do you have to set goals to get things done? Do you require some indirect supervision? Are there times you require direct supervision?

3) How much do you know about guns, weapons, or other implements which could be used against you? Do you know how to protect yourself, regardless of your body size and strength?

READING

Fortunately, the rest of the week went without major incidents, calamities, injuries, or disasters. Tuesday, Wednesday, and Thursday included the usual trips to school, the one hour of required drug education, and even our weekly visits from the main detention's chaplain. The return to daily monotony freed my coworkers and me to focus on our additional assigned duties. I took advantage of the calm to organize the properties room, separating the materials that were owned by escapees from over six months ago, and preparing those items for donation to a local shelter. Sarah was working on organizing outings and preparing for the annual Christmas party we provided for those unfortunate kids who couldn't convince a judge to release them, so they were forced to stay with us over the holidays. Every employee knew that these moments of calm needed to be used to their fullest.

I continued to keep an eye on Curtis, as he was my current special project. Curtis continued to show positive silent leadership skills among the other youths. I wanted to find a way to help him once he got out of this group home, to continue to lead others in positive directions. But I knew better than to push my luck. It was very difficult for us to keep in contact with these kids once they got out. Technically, that was the responsibility of their probation officers, but each officer worked on over 100 cases and had new ones assigned daily.

I made sure that I talked one-on-one with Curtis at least once a day. We would talk about his home life, his little brother, little sister, anything I could use to help get me further under his armor. I asked him why he was always picking on his baby sister. Curtis was visibly offended by my question. "I love my sister and don't you forget it!" He went on to tell me that he watched how girls were treated like dirt on the street. A girl was not looked on as a person, but as an opportunity for sex. They were always talked down to, usually physically abused and often raped. He wanted her to keep as far away from his lifestyle as possible. I asked Curtis if he wanted to get out of the street life if he could. "You just don't understand, man," came his answer. "You can't just leave a gang. These letters on my hands don't fade! You try to walk away, and it will follow you. You tell everybody, you ain't going to hang no more, and they follow you. You tell other gangs you ain't gonna fight for them no more, and they beat the crap outta yah. I've tried man, but the only way out of this life is in a box in the ground."

"And if you don't quit you will be either in and out of jails for the rest of your life, or in a box in the ground," I responded.

"I know, but every time I try to quit, it follows me. I have tried to walk away many times, and every time I get the shit beaten out of me or my homies need me to get them out of a spot. The only time I am safe is when I am with my homies."

"But when you walk with your homies, you are not safe," I respond. "Every time you walk with them there is a good chance that someone will do a drive-by on all of you. It's much easier to ID you when you are in group."

"But, if I am with them, I know they will look out for me."

"It's not hard to look out for you if you are dead."

"If I die man, then I know my homies will get revenge for me," he answered without even thinking about what he was saying.

"What will you care about revenge?" I asked. "You will be food for worms. And what about the innocent people that get caught in the crossfire?"

"Man, there ain't no innocent people on the streets. Everyone is guilty of something!"

"Does that include your sister, Angelie? What if she gets shot? Is she guilty of something?" I asked.

I had him! I knew that I had earned my pay when I was able to make a youth think, if just for one moment. He sat there silently and looked into himself. I sat there and let him think. He finally responded, "I hate it when you do that to me."

"It's my job. It's time for you to start thinking about how your street activities will affect her." I got up to continue with my other duties.

By the end of the week I was almost ready to empty out most of the storage room. I had eight bags of clothes and personal items that had been abandoned, and I was sick of looking at them. I was glad on Wednesday when I got permission to take these bags down the street to a local homeless shelter. I volunteered three youths, and each of us carried two large bags. We probably looked like poor Santa's helpers or that we were homeless ourselves. It only took five minutes to get rid of what took two years to pile up. Now I could look forward to starting a new inventory system during the weekend.

I also got to listen as my three volunteers described to everyone else what they had just done. The boys were not usually permitted to go downstairs into the basement, so the stories my volunteers told about what was down there were very humorous to me. Then they told everybody about the things that we had taken to the shelter. There was an outcry from my charges about giving away items that they felt they should have had a chance at getting. I informed them that state law required us to either give them to a registered charity or throw them out in the trash. I could also have told them that most of this stuff was total trash, but I knew that they would not believe me. I was glad to leave this behind for my day and a half off. After eight shifts in five days, I needed a few extra hours of sleep.

When I returned from my days off the house was still well under control. The journal read like a list of instructed entries. No riots, no fires, no fights, just head counts, activities, meals ordered or arriving, and shifts changing. It had been calm. The only changes were the release of two kids and the arrival of two more. These new youths were small enough not to want to get into trouble or even be noticed. This weekend had the makings for easy shifts. The calendar showed four releases for tomorrow, but today was clear.

When Mike arrived at 0800 hours we agreed not to wake the boys for another half hour. All the communication it took was his waving a cigarette at me as he walked out the front door for a smoke. Mike could use few words when he wanted. Besides, breakfast was late again.

I took advantage of the free time to go downstairs to create my new inventory list. It only took me fifteen minutes to finish it, since I was not being interrupted. By getting this done early, it freed me from this job for the rest of the day. It also meant that I did not hear the doorbell when breakfast arrived. Mike came looking for me just to make sure I had not abandoned him to his fate or was not taken hostage by any of our charges.

Once breakfast had arrived there was little reason for letting the boys sleep in any further. We could tell from the sounds coming from the second floor that at least three of the twelve were already awake and moving about. Mike started the ritual of preparing breakfast while I went to awaken everyone. I could almost guess who was already awake and ready to go, vs. who was still in their bed with the sheets over their head. It was no surprise that Curtis was sitting on his bed fully dressed, staring out his window. "Whatcha thinking about?" I asked.

Curtis looked up and through me. "Nothin' much."

"You wouldn't happen to be thinking about your trial on Tuesday?" I asked, knowing what the answer would be.

"Uh-huh." I knew better than to expect much conversation from him this early in the morning. I just continued on my morning rounds, greeting those who were awake, and awakening those who greeted me with a snore. Breakfast was quiet, as those who were awake were thinking about their own issues, and those who were asleep did not want to be bothered. The only real conversation was on whether to watch the local college game or to go out and play ball. As a heavy rain started to hit the windows, the college game won the debate, and the room again returned to quiet murmuring. Even when I put out the chore lists, everyone quietly went to do their chores, rather than making a complaint. The only sound that broke the pattern was the vacuum cleaner moving about the carpets and the moving of furniture. I grabbed the morning paper and let the kids do their chores. Mike came in to the office and grabbed the sports page. We sat back and enjoyed the lack of annoyances.

The chores were completed and the game came on. The rest of the day continued quietly. Mike and I took turns doing those duties for which we were responsible. We all sat in the living room and watched the ball game, while I read my paper, Mike had the sports section, and some of the clients were reading one of Mike's fishing magazines. Everything was quiet until the two new kids came across an ad in one of Mike's fishing magazines for a hunting rifle.

Each kid started to brag about the different guns they claimed to own. One of them bragged about the number of street lights he had shot out. I had heard enough. "I bet you stood on the street near the light when you shot."

"Yeah, how'd you know?" one of the kids asked.

"You look that stupid," I started. "Have you ever heard the phrase, 'what goes up, must come down?'"

"Yeah. What's your point?"

"When you shoot a bullet up at a lamp, it has to come down somewhere. It can come right back at you. Have you thought about that?" I asked.

"No," He answered in a hesitant voice.

"I'll bet you don't even know the simplest things about gun care," I continued. "When was the last time you cleaned a gun? Have you ever oiled one? Field stripped one? You don't even know what cleaning and field stripping are."

"I do too, and I've watched my dad do it many times," came his defensive answer. I knew that I did not have to respond to this comment, as he had shown everybody that he had just shown how much of a fool he really was.

I knew that I should not say much more but I could just not restrain myself. "Wait a minute, aren't you the one who is doing time here for shooting the neighbor's waterbed, when the gun you were holding went off by accident?"

Everyone started to hoot and holler. If this kid was older, I would not have embarrassed him in front of the others. But with younger kids, I would try to drive a wedge between them and the older kids. If these younger clients could learn not to like these other kids now, they might not want to get into further trouble. The laughter broke up what would have otherwise been a boring shift. Now I could go home feeling that I might have accomplished something. I did not want to embarrass him more than was necessary, but I also wanted to get him to think about how stupid his actions were. If he thought that bragging about owning a gun was going to get him respect from his "peers," I was going to make sure that he learned that respect is earned in better ways than being stupid for others' entertainment.

Sunday showed promise of being just as slow. The only real difference was the release of four of the kids. Our two youngest kids were scheduled to be released at nine o'clock. When I arrived they were already sitting in the living room waiting for their parents to show up. When one set of parents arrived, we would have them sign for their kid and let them leave. We had already dealt with their property and made sure that they had not damaged their rooms in any way. As they walked out the door, each staff member would say something about not wanting to see them back here ever again.

For the second youth of the morning, I had a point to make. I called him into the office and told him to sit down in front of my desk. "The reason I called you in here is that I wanted to talk about our discussion from yesterday."

"Yeah, what about it?" he asked in a sarcastic voice, hiding his face from me.

"Since it sounds like you are bound and determined to come back here again, don't let it be for a firearms violation. If you keep pulling shit like that, you may not ever come back here again."

"Yeah, next time they won't catch me."

"They won't have to. You'll be sitting there in a pool of your own blood waiting for them to come and save your sorry ass. The only question that they will have to answer is whether to call for an ambulance or a body bag. Think about it. You have the choice to find other things to do, or you can kill yourself. Either way does not matter to me. If you keep it up, you will either be dead, or back here. If you are dead, I don't have to deal with you. If you come back again, hell, you'll just be keeping me employed. But if someone else gets hit with one of your bullets, then I will care. You have no right to take someone else's life. So if you want to play with guns and kill yourself, that's your choice. If you kill someone else doing it, then to *HELL* with you. *NOW*, get out of my office."

The kid was still shaking when his parents came to get him. His mother commented on it, and Mike told her that I had just put the fear of God into him, and that her son should be fine in a few hours. After they left, Mike and I had our usual argument about guns.

Mike had grown up on the streets and had seen a number of his friends shot with guns. He had served in the military and seen highly trained personnel shoot themselves by accident. Mike did not like guns at all. I also had grown up around guns. I had been taught how to handle them properly, how to clean them, and how to use them. I looked on them as a tool that needed to be handled very carefully. For Mike, guns were of the Devil's making, and should be treated as such. He and I would argue on this subject for five to ten minutes, and then agree to disagree, rather than letting it get to us. We had a job to do and ten detainees to wake up.

The day continued to be calm and uneventful. The kids woke up with little event and breakfast and chores were completed smoothly, with only the minimal required complaining. Since the local team was playing Philadelphia, there was no point in even asking what people wanted to do. I just turned on the pre-game show and sat back. We did not talk much until the game started. During the game it was not acceptable to have a conversation during a play. A person might let out an exclamation of frustration or cheer, but you did not want to ruin the game for others. During the commercials it was fun to watch some of the kids and Mike discussing, recreating and second-guessing the events on the field 3000 miles away. Sometimes it was hard to remember that we were supposed to be watching these detained juvenile criminals, and were not a group of friends together for a day of armchair quarterbacking.

The afternoon went about the same. Everything went smoothly during the games. The kids who were scheduled to be released all left on time or were picked up on time. The only rough spot of the day came when quiet hour arrived as the fourth quarter started. Most knew better than to argue, so lethargically everyone headed to their rooms. As Curtis passed me on the stairs, he finally gave me a hint as to what was bothering him. "You don't think David is going to show for my trial, do you?" I realized he was asking about his friend who was supposed to come and explain how Curtis was not the guilty one. "I don't know," was all I felt comfortable saying. Curtis and I would talk again before the trial, but for now he had to come to terms with the reality that his homie was about to let him down again. I let Curtis go up to his room and rest for ten minutes, then I moved to follow him.

Walking into Curtis's room, I asked if I could come in. Curtis made a gesture I translated as he did not care if I came or left, so I sat down. To get a conversation started I asked, "Why does it bother you that your gang bro might not show up for your hearing?"

"Man, he's supposed to be my bro. I risked my life for him in street fights. He is supposed to be there for me. I'd put my life on the line for him; where is he now when I need him?"

"Curtis, these are important questions you are asking," I started. "Do you really want to put your life on the line for someone who won't show up to help you, even when they have nothing to lose?"

Curtis just sat there and looked at the floor. I just let him think about what we had just said. A major part of what Curtis believed in his life was now being questioned. Curtis was thinking about his life, his "family" and his future. Finally, he looked up at me. "I need some time to face this myself. I just need some time to think."

I got up from my chair and looked at Curtis as I left. Before I turned my back on him and my work day I turned to remind Curtis, "Think hard about this, Curtis. Not just for me or yourself, but for your mother, brother and baby sister."

I closed the door to his room and went to get ready to go home. I looked at Mike and just nodded my head, yes. Mike understood everything without a word being said.

Curtis had finally started to think for himself. Now it was up to him. If he really wanted to leave the gang I could help him, but it was his decision and actions that would count now. Only Curtis could make the day-to-day choices which could either build a future life for himself, or bring him to his own death.

ADDITIONAL INFORMATION

Individual vs. Group Activities

One major part of the equation on how you work with these youths is whether you can work with these as individuals or groups. Each method has benefits and drawbacks. Each method must be used in specific circumstances and should be avoided in others. The use of an approach in the wrong environment can create unsettling embarrassment for an older client, or put other youths at risk of harm.

A group environment is one where you are working with more than one client at one time. These need not be formal, scheduled, and planned group activities. Group sessions can take place anytime you are presented an opportunity to teach a lesson or make an example. As illustrated in the story, this can happen at any time, coming from a casual conversation, a television commercial, or even a side comment made by a youth.

There are many benefits to teaching and counseling in groups. First, group lessons allow you to work with all of the youths; thus you know where everybody is and what they are doing. Second, you can take advantage of the knowledge or misconceptions of many youths at once. Third, you may be able to take advantage of peer learning, if you have older youths who have already learned the lesson you are trying to teach. Kids are more likely to accept difficult lessons from each other, rather than from an adult counselor, teacher, or parent.

However, group teaching and counseling comes with some inherent risks. First, you had better know the subject matter and the youths' perceptions; otherwise the youths will take over the lesson and the session could become counterproductive. Second, it is more difficult to hold the interests of many youths in a conversation, rather than one. Third, it will be more difficult to get youths to open up and speak honestly for themselves in a group. Fourth, if a youth does say something personal, or you bring out a personal fact about a youth, you will risk embarrassing them in front of their peers and alienating them. Fifth, if you do not have another staff member or all of the clients' attention, there will be some youths who are not being supervised.

The other side of counseling is an individual approach. These sessions usually take place in a more isolated location so you are aware of interruptions and can reduce the chances of others listening to what you say. These sessions can take place at a planned time or whenever a youth is isolated for a period of time. Individual counseling has many benefits. First, youths are more likely to talk openly about more personal topics than they might with others present. Second, individual time can give a youth the special time they might need to work out a problem. Third, the risk of interruption by uninterested parties can be better controlled.

However, there are risks of working with youths one-on-one. Primarily, the more you work with a youth, the closer you may come emotionally to that youth. Some youths will try to use this bond against you by trying to get away with violations other youths cannot. Second, when you are working with one youth in an isolated environment you have no one else who can confirm what happened. A youth could accuse you of making inappropriate actions toward them, or just say you gave them bad advice and you will have no witnesses to state what did or did not happen. This is a serious liability issue from which you must protect yourself. Finally, while you are working with one youth, someone must watch all of the other youths in the program. In the program described in this book, there are two staff members and twelve youths. This would mean that one staff member would be responsible for watching and controlling the behavior of eleven youths. Therefore, this method can only be used in controlled situations.

There are numerous factors which should be considered when deciding whether to work one-on-one or in a group environment. The first question you need to ask is, "What are the demands on your human resources?" If you are the only staff member and you have six youths for whom you are responsible, then you will always need to work with a group approach so you can monitor all of these youths.

The second limitation of your approach is the physical environment. The best environment for individual counseling is a room with a window facing into the rest of the program; thus, others can look in and see what is occurring. The window also allows you to look out and see if you are needed by your coworker. If you do not have a window, you can leave the door open, but this means that your conversation can be overheard.

The third issue that you will need to consider is the potential of the other youths in your program. If you have even one youth who has demonstrated the potential to harm someone else, to physically damage the property of the program, or violate the rules of the program, then you need to make sure that this specific youth is properly supervised. Just the presence of this youth will limit your ability to perform one-on-one counseling.

When thinking about counseling or teaching a lesson, be aware of the environment in which you are working. Does the lesson call for group or individual approaches? Do you have an appropriate location for this lesson? Are there enough staff for you to take the time to teach the lesson or provide the counseling? In time, you will learn to answer these questions by experience and may even add a few questions of your own to the list.

What are you talking about?

In any youth program the kids are going to talk to each other. Even if you are not involved in the conversation, as a staff member, it is still part of your job to know what they are talking about. To make this more difficult, the youths will use street talk or other lingo. As a youth worker, you need to understand when what they are saying that might be a threat or a potential violation of program rules. By understanding youth conversations, you add a serious level of control into your program.

An example of a conversation you need to understand is when youths are talking about weapons. First of all, everything that sounds like a weapon is a threat. A .38 special is a small gun that can easily be hidden in a pocket. A "p-38" is the old military lingo for a small hand can opener, or a small German World War II pistol. If you were ignorant of this information a youth could not only embarrass you in front of the other youths, but could undermine your authority.

Another reason for listening carefully to youth talk is to understand what they might be using against you. Youths may give hints in casual conversations about activities in which they may be taking part. One youth telling another that he has a staple may appear harmless, but what he may be saying is that he has a staple which can be used to start a fire if placed in an electrical plug. Listen to what is being said and you may be able to avoid future problems in the program.

MAJOR POINTS

1) Observe what is going on around you before you decide to use group or individualized approaches to working with the youths in your program.

2) Learn to listen to conversations for possible threats and inappropriate conversations. Learn street terminology for guns and weapons, and learn how these weapons can be used against you. Learn how everyday items can be used as weapons, threats and implements of destruction.

3) Even if you are a pacifist, take the time to learn about conflict. Become comfortable with conflict. PEACEMAKERS WORK WITHIN ENVIRONMENTS OF CONFLICT!!!

CLASS ACTIVITIES

1) The instructor will give the class five objects. Students, as individuals, will examine these objects and determine which can be used as a weapon and how. As a class, share your answers. Listen carefully to how others would use these

objects. How do other students' experiences relate to their ideas? As a class, talk about how an unsettled youth might use these objects and what can be done to counter these threats.

2) At home each student walks around where they live. Each student will write a two-page paper examining obvious and hidden threats to their safety. This paper should include possible remedies to these threats.

3) As a class discuss what factors should influence your decision to use group or individualized approaches to working with various groups of kids. Create various scenarios and examine which approach might work best given the resources available and the needs of the clients described.

Chapter 11
Trial by Fire

QUESTIONS TO THINK ABOUT AS YOU READ
1) Is justice served by heavy use of plea bargains? Could courts handle the work load without them?
2) What is the role of probation? How does this compare to other social service organizations?
3) How close or distant should you keep your emotions toward the youths with whom you are working?
4) How and when should your personal morals affect how you do your duties?

READING
Tuesday finally came. Curtis was letting some of his nervousness show. He was edgy all day. When he rarely spoke, it was only in short and blunt statements. Most of the kids avoided unnecessary contact with him. This was not the same Curtis who had been so cocky walking to court two weeks ago. This was a boy who knew that he was in trouble and that he had no one else to look to for help. His only hope was that his friend might show up, out of nowhere.

As we walked to court that afternoon, Curtis tried to put on his confident face, but there were cracks all around it. I could tell that he was nervous. He knew that if the judge recognized him, he might be sent away for a while. Not because stealing a cell phone was such a high crime; I had seen kids only get two to four days for stealing and totaling someone's new car. Curtis was nervous because he was known before this court, and more than one judge had threatened that if they ever saw him again, his sentence would be measured in months or years, not weeks or days.

After we passed security and were signing in, Curtis's attorney approached. "After you have signed in, please come and see me in that room over there." He gestured to one of the small conference rooms. Curtis signed the paperwork, and we moved quickly to get out of the press of people who had no idea where they were going. Curtis sat down at the table, and his attorney continued to look over the file.

"We have a problem," the lawyer started. "Your alibi was arrested yesterday in California. Not only does he have an outstanding warrant there, he also is suspected of attempted homicide. There is no way we will be able to get him here to testify anytime soon. I could ask for a delay of trial, and then use it to plea bargain. Do you have a problem with that?"

Curtis just shrugged his shoulders. I knew that he was preparing himself mentally for this. He knew that one more offense on his record would not make that much of a difference. However, he also wanted to get out of detention, and a plea bargain offered the quickest way out. Both Curtis and I knew that only one in fifty juvenile cases ever actually goes to trial.

"What you gonna try for?" Curtis asked.

"I think that we can probably get you out today, if you let me play my cards," his attorney responded.

This concerned me because I was finally making progress with Curtis, and I wanted just one more week to try to help him to start planning his exit from gang life. In this one week I might be able to get him connected with more alternative programs and activities. I knew that his attorney's focus was to get Curtis the best deal he could. It was a rare defense attorney who would argue that a youth needed one more minute in juvenile detention than they had already served.

His lawyer continued, "You have been in detention for about a month now, and if we plead guilty to Theft Three, the longest sentence is only two weeks. Even if the judge wanted to keep you in for longer, they would be hard pressed to justify it on just a Theft Three charge."

Curtis nodded, and slowly rose to leave the room. His attorney reminded him that this was not yet a done deal, and that he would have to see what he could pull off with the prosecutor. We went to find a seat where we could wait comfortably. A number of detention personnel walked past us during our wait and commented sarcastically, "Hard job you got there."

"You want to trade. I can take your eight to five hours and salary, and you can work sixteen hour days on the weekend." I took their quick refusals as proof to my feeling that I had earned a few hours of ease once in a while. Curtis just ignored their comments and sat quietly ignoring all of us. I occasionally asked him if he wanted something to read, and he just gestured, "No."

An hour and a half later his attorney again signaled for us to join him in a conference room. "I have talked with the prosecutor. She was not willing to agree to Theft Three. However, she is willing to agree to let you plead to a Theft Two charge, with time served. This means you could walk out today, as long as the judge goes along. Remember, the judge does not have to follow our suggestions, so by pleading guilty to Theft Two, you are only improving your chances of getting out today. There are no promises that you will walk out of the court free."

Curtis shook his head in understanding. At this point he just wanted to get the day over with. I had never seen him look so uncomfortable. We got up and went back into the waiting room. The attorney joined us after conferring with the prosecutor. Half an hour later we were still waiting when we were finally called into Courtroom Three.

As we walked into the room, Curtis's mood changed suddenly. I looked up on the bench and realized that the judge who was presiding was a fill-in for a regular judge who was on vacation. This judge might not have seen Curtis before and might not feel the strong compulsion to throw the book at him.

After everyone was seated in their proper places, the prosecutor asked for the tape recorder to be turned on so that she might begin. Now everything went according to a strict formula. Curtis was in his element. He remembered to hunch his shoulders over and try to look repentant. If only he could get that silly smirk off his face.

"Is something funny, Mr. Jones?" the judge asked in a controlled deep voice. The smirk disappeared from Curtis's face. The judge indicated to the prosecutor to begin the proceedings. The prosecutor remained seated and gave a speech which she had almost memorized about arranging a plea bargain. Then it was the judge's turn to read off the standard set of questions. To each question Curtis answered, "Yes."

"Have you discussed this plea bargain with your attorney?"

"Did he explain that I do not have to follow any of the recommendations in sentencing?"

"Has anyone made any promises or threats to get you to agree to this plea?"

"No," Curtis whispered.

Only after he answered all of these questions, did the judge agree to accept the plea of guilty to Theft Two. Then the three parties to the trial made their recommendations on sentencing to the judge. The prosecutor asked for the maximum permitted by law, four weeks. This was no surprise, since this meant that Curtis would still be released today. Curtis's own attorney made a show of it asking for a light sentence of only two weeks. Everyone in the room knew that this argument meant nothing, but he had to do it for the court record. Besides,

Curtis could then have his community service hours reduced for the extra days he had already served. The only surprise came when the probation officer prepared to give her recommendation.

"Your honor, I would ask that Curtis not be assigned any community supervision time. He has a clear record of refusing to cooperate with me and my predecessors. If you do sentence him to any supervision time, I am convinced that I will be before this court again in a few weeks with a probation violation charge."

The judge apparently heard everything and had agreed with the recommendations. Rather than assigning a specific sentence, the judge ordered that he be given "time served" and no community supervision time was given. Curtis would be walking out of court knowing that in a few hours he would be free. Curtis tried hard not to look joyful as the final papers were signed. I knew he was thinking, "I can be home in time for dinner."

As I walked Curtis back to the house, I again began to see the cocky Curtis appear, the same Curtis I had seen in the early morning those few weeks ago. As we walked up the hill, Curtis started to think about what he was going to eat as soon as he was released. No sooner had we gotten back to the house than I began to check Curtis out of the program. I had him go collect his belongings from upstairs, while I got his paperwork in order.

I was preparing the paperwork when the phone call came ordering us to release Curtis to himself immediately. I went to the stairs and shouted for him to hurry up. I could tell that he was running around upstairs telling everyone that he was finally going to be released after four weeks with us. It took him a few more minutes, but I got him downstairs and signed out. Curtis was almost in shock with the idea that he was going to be walking out our door in a few minutes. He did everything he could to make the procedure go quicker. He had organized his pants and shirts, and five minutes after he entered the office, he was on his way to walk out the door. I made sure to comment to Curtis that he should make an effort not to return to detention. I knew he was not listening! Curtis was free to leave, and free to get on with his life. I also knew that Curtis might be already thinking about the type of trouble he could get into that evening. All the work that the other staff and I had done with Curtis would now be tested. I only hoped that he might continue to think about his brother and sister when deciding on his own actions.

The rest of the shift was anti-climactic after the release. I just sat at my desk documenting what had just happened. I just wanted one more week to work with Curtis and maybe get him connected with a few more service agencies. Only hope or fear kept me from believing that I would be seeing Curtis again.

It was a Tuesday afternoon, two months after Curtis's release, before I heard his last name again. He was not spending time in our program, but rather it was his younger brother Luther who sat before my desk while I reviewed the rules with him. I had been working at detention now for four months, and I was one of the more senior staff members. To see a younger brother was no surprise to me, but this was Curtis's brother, and I was curious about how Curtis was faring.

Luther was more than happy to brag about the trouble his brother was causing. As I heard the details, I knew that all of my efforts to get Curtis to think about others did not make any long-term changes in his behavior. He went right back to causing trouble the day he got out of our program. Curtis had been released only to be arrested again for Minor in Possession of Alcohol.

"My brother was just released yesterday," Luther boasted. I asked him if he wanted to be just like his brother and Luther asked me, "What's wrong with that?"

"Well," I started, "if Curtis keeps up his tricks, he may find himself dead if he doesn't watch it."

"Yeah, right. My brother ain't gonna die. Others might get shot at or shoot at him, but Curtis has never even been hit. I'll be just like him."

"That's what I am afraid of," I thought to myself. I knew what the streets were like. I watched as my coworkers asked for days off for funeral leave. I feared how soon it was before it would be my turn.

Early Wednesday morning, the next day, the phone call I had feared came. I had already been on duty for eight hours, but I could recognize the crying voice of Ms. Natasha Jones. I could barely understand her through her tears, but her sobs communicated more than words ever could. She wanted to talk, and I was there to listen as she told me the story for fifteen minutes. I had long ago forgotten any anger I had with Curtis for how he treated me on my first day. Besides, this was a mother talking about her oldest son. Before I hung up, I was also crying.

Curtis had been shot and killed. The night before he snuck out of his bedroom window and was looking for his homies. He made the mistake of taking a shortcut through an alley. It was the last mistake he ever made. Someone thought that he was trying to sell on their turf, and shot him five times. Curtis was dead before he hit the ground. All I could do was offer my condolences to Ms. Jones and tell her that I would inform Luther as soon as I could. I also told her that I would see what I could do about getting Luther released for the funeral.

I remember the feeling of my foot slowly touching each of those stairs as I walked up to tell Luther about his brother. Each step pained me as if it was my own death to which I was walking. Luther had been assigned to the same room as Curtis, and it was Curtis's face I expected and wanted to see behind the door. I opened his door, and Luther looked up at me from his bed. He had been awakened by the squeak of his door opening. I pulled up a chair to his bed and sat down. Luther took a look at my face and knew that it was bad news. "Curtis?" he asked.

I could not think of any soft way to say it, and the words tumbled out of my mouth like a drunk stagger. "He was dead before he even reached the ground. The funeral will be on Saturday." I had wanted to break the news more gracefully, but the full impact of the moment overtook me and we both sat there crying. My coworker heard the noise upstairs and came to see what the crying was about. I could not answer his questions; it was all I could do to say, "Curtis." We sat in the room together either crying or thinking silent thoughts.

That morning Sarah tried to arrange for Luther to have a pass for the funeral, and for me to have the day off to attend. The boss was not pleased that I felt a need to go to one of our clients' funerals, but she also understood that Curtis and I had worked together, and that I felt I had made some progress with him. Juvenile detention finally found a judge who would agree to sign an order, but only under the strictest of terms. The judge's order read that I was to escort Luther to his mother's apartment and to the funeral. The order actually specified me, so no one else could take my place at the funeral. In this way, Sarah made sure I would not miss even an hour of work, Luther would be permitted to attend the funeral, and my boss could not object to my following a judge's specific order.

Luther was not pleased that he was going to have a "babysitter" for his own brother's funeral. I pointed out to him that I was going, and it was his choice if he wanted to come along. He told me, "You do know, my bro thought you were crazy. He could not understand why you bothered spending so much time talking to him."

I look over at Luther and asked, "And what do you think?"

He looked down at our ugliest carpet and held his thoughts for a few minutes. Finally he voiced, "I don't know what to think anymore."

On Saturday, I arrived at work dressed in my formal clothes. Everyone was well behaved, even for a weekend. Everyone knew what happened and no one wanted to get either the staff or Luther upset. At ten o'clock Luther and I left the building. Luther gave me directions to his apartment building. After tearfully hugging his mother, Luther went to change into a suit his mother had bought for him. While he changed, I tried to help Ms. Jones with the preparations for after the funeral. I knew that I was supposed to be watching Luther, but I also knew that this family needed help to get through this day.

Luther took half an hour to get dressed and join us in the main area of his mother's small apartment. Everything was in order, and Ms. Jones asked me to keep an eye on Luther and Angelie, while she went to go finish preparing herself for this day. I knew that there was really nothing any parent could do to prepare themselves for an event like this. Luther started to look at his sister playing with her toys. She barely understood what happened, but she knew about today and she was dealing with it in her own way. Luther just stood there and watched his sister. "Does she look up to you, like you looked up to Curtis?" I asked. Luther did not answer. I could tell he was thinking very hard, and that his reality was being shaken to its foundation.

When Ms. Jones joined us, it was time to go. She asked me to join them riding in a friend's car. She knew that Luther had to stay with me, but I think she also wanted to have another adult with her to help with the children. Ms. Jones was a proud African-American woman who had just lost her oldest gem. She wanted to be strong, but she was going to need help. I sat next to Luther in the car. He later told me that members of the church had all pitched in to help pay for the funeral, since his mother could never have afforded anything like this.

I was pleasantly surprised by the reception I received at the church. Many of the adults asked how I knew Curtis, and either their children or I explained. Although Curtis was dead, I did not want to remind these people that his death might be considered partially the result of the failure of my efforts. Many of the teenagers at the church were known to me in one way or another. In the front of the altar was Curtis, lying in his coffin. Ms. Jones asked me to come with her as she said goodbye to her son.

As we walked up to the coffin I realized that Luther was over talking to some of his homies without adult supervision. I was torn between my official duties and my personal religious duties. But I had been raised to believe that it was the paramount duty of a moral person to console the bereaved. It was this obligation which made me decide to stay by Ms. Jones and hold her up as she again broke down crying. I should have been watching Luther and keeping him out of trouble, but this was something I knew I needed to do.

Besides, here I was trying not to look at Curtis. I kept hoping he would just open his eyes and yell out, "Fooled yahh." However, deeper in my heart I was asking myself if there was anything else I might have done that would have changed Curtis's life for the better. I only wished I could hear him telling me that he had made his own choices, despite my efforts and not because of them. I tried to lift myself out of my own depressed thoughts, by looking over to Ms. Jones.

When I looked over to her other side I noticed someone helping me hold her. There was Luther kneeling next to his mother in quiet prayer. I was relieved to see this. We looked at each other. I considered trying to make another point about his life to him, but chose to keep my mouth shut. Together we helped his mother to her feet and led her to a seat in the front of the church.

The reverend entered the room and came over to talk to us. The reverend spoke first to Ms. Jones and then to Luther. "Luther, I know that some of your friends will encourage you to get revenge for your brother's death. I will not give you a sermon on the evils of revenge. All I want you to do is ask yourself, 'Are you worthy to make God's judgment?'" With that the reverend walked away. Luther just sat there visibly shaking. I was beginning to believe that some good might come out of this tragedy.

I was not Christian, so Mike had tried to prepare me for what a Southern Baptist funeral was like. There were a number of differences which I would have otherwise not been prepared for. The hardest difference was the open coffin. For me it was considered disrespectful to look upon the face of the dead. I just sat there and felt like Curtis was accusing me of failing him. This was the same young man who was so full of life the last time I saw him. Now he just lay there . . . cold and dead.

The ride to the cemetery was hard for all of us. Luther and his mother were still crying. When we arrived, everyone walked slowly over to the open grave. Off to the side I saw a face I recognized. It was Community Officer Murphy. I walked over and asked him why he was there. He told me, "Word on the street is that the shooter might be here and there might be a revenge shooting, or that there might be another drive-by shooting at the funeral. I was ordered to stand here and look like deterrent."

Together we stood there and watched as Curtis was lowered into the ground. I watched Luther pick up the first shovel full of soil and drop it on to the coffin which held his idol, his mentor, his older brother. The look on his face showed the conflict being waged inside of his fourteen-year-old mind. I continued to watch the scene around the grave, and was surprised to see Luther walk slowly over to Officer Murphy and myself.

Luther spoke quietly: "Murph, can you to do me a favor? Lose this for me." Luther reached into his suit pocket and pulled something out. Into Murphy's hands, Luther placed a small fully loaded pistol. Luther looked at me and answered my silent questions. "One of my friends gave it to me when you were over helping my mother, doing what I should have been doing. I suppose I'm going to be in real trouble now."

Officer Murphy and I looked at each other with surprise at how things were turning out. Officer Murphy closed his fingers around the weapon. "Son, you can't get in trouble for doing the right thing."

It took me a moment to get my thoughts together. Looking at the old worn-out weapon enclosed in Officer Murphy's hand and the expression of concern on the young man's face I needed to think. Thoughts filled my head of the various paths Luther's life could take either following his brother into an early grave. Based on the cold reality of Luther's momentary decision, I could only answer, "Actually Luther, now I think you might just be OK."

ADDITIONAL INFORMATION

What is Probation?

The role of probation is to make sure that a person who is either on pre-trial release or was found guilty and has been sentenced follows the court orders that have been placed on them. These conditions are for a set period of time and are usually very specific. One of the usual conditions is that the person in question not be accused or convicted of another crime.

Since the average probation counselor has a large case load, they cannot perfectly monitor their clients to help the clients avoid violations. Once a violation has occurred, the probation officer will bring this violation to the attention of the court where appropriate consequences can be implemented. Since one of the most common violations of probation occurs when someone does not contact their probation counselor, many violations can take a long time before any consequence is realized by the offender.

Reality

This chapter could have turned out very differently than it did. First of all, Luther could have killed someone. The staff member was not providing the proper observation and Luther came in contact with a loaded gun. Had Luther chosen to use the gun, the staff member might not only been fired, but could also have been subject to civil liabilities. Remember, when you are working with high-risk youths, even the smallest choices you make can have a real effect on how a situation turns out.

In the end, it was Luther who made the choice. He could have been hardened by the death of his brother and started to look for revenge. In the end, what youth workers, teachers, social workers and probation counselors do is provide other options to our clients. It is up to the clients to make the choices which may either help or hurt them. All Josh did was model one type of behavior, which Luther chose to adopt.

This is the challenge that awaits you working with at-risk and high-risk youths. First, you must control the youths in your program. Second, you must present a model of behavior for your clients to follow. Finally, you try to give the youths other options to the behaviors that got them in trouble in the first place. Then it is up to the youths to take advantage of what is offered. Only the youth can make the moment-to-moment choices which create a change in lifestyle.

Life Cycle of a Youth Worker

Most youth workers who are working directly and intensively with at-risk and high-risk youths have recently graduated from college with an associate's or bachelor's degree. They are younger, in their twenties, and are generally optimistic about their lives and the impact they can make on the world. Ahead of them are a number of different career paths, which their degrees, personalities and a measure of chance will create.

The degree is the easiest to explain. Obviously, if you are leaving college with a teaching certificate, you are expecting to be a schoolteacher. If you studied criminal justice, you might be expecting a career in law enforcement, corrections, law, or probation. Those with degrees in psychology, sociology, or anthropology have a wider range of jobs available to them when they graduate, but will have to be able to explain how their training has prepared them for the particular job for which they are applying.

During the first years of a person's career, they will learn about the realities of their career choice. This hands-on education will likely affect the person's view on the world and their place in it. Experience in this field tends to make people less optimistic and more realistic or even pessimistic. While these changes will affect the person's effectiveness on the job, it will also change the worker's view of their career choice.

This is where a youth worker's personality will affect their career path. The personality of many youth workers is directly challenged by these changes in perspective. These people can adapt to what they have learned on the job, change their own approach, or get out of the field. Personal conflicts between the expectation of the job and your expectations of yourself can make working with high-risk kids very difficult. These kids know when you are lying to yourself, and will either call you on your hypocrisy or try to use it to their own advantage.

Some youth workers will adapt their personality to the realities with which they are working. They will realize that they can only work so hard, and that they must also have a life outside their career. These people will take vacations and sabbaticals from work, have other outside activities and take part in family and community events. These people will survive more than a few years in their jobs and careers.

Mid-career evaluation can actually occur at any time in one's life. This is a time when a person questions what he or she is doing, where he or she is, and what he or she may become. There are many effects this can have on one's career. Some leave stable jobs, experiment with other possibilities and then return to where they started or work in other positions they find more rewarding.

Others cannot experiment because they have families to support or they are in jobs which reward them for staying for a few more years. Such rewards are more common in teaching or police fields where some retirement plans allow for retirement at any age after twenty or thirty years of service. However, these careers also have different areas in which one can move around to find new challenges. Teachers can take coursework during the summer and add specializations which permit them to work with different populations of youths. Police have different units they can work in, or they may get promoted into different levels of administration.

Yet another option for those who are questioning their career choices is to start working for themselves. After years of working with high-risk youths, many workers develop special skills and expertise. They also may have made professional contacts that can help them set up a firm of their own, get social services contracts with the government or other agencies, and succeed on their own. This will give them the freedom to create their own policies, rules and only take those cases with which they want to work. The risk is that they must have enough work to support themselves, and all risks, financial and legal, are also their own.

The final major indicator of one's career path is chance. Even with the best degree and a winning personality, new graduates can find it difficult to find a job if the economic conditions in their geographic location are not good. Chance can also provide a new graduate with career opportunities they might not have thought about during their training. There may be such a high demand for police officers that a graduate with a degree in psychology may find themselves in law enforcement. Be prepared for whatever options life may present to you.

MAJOR POINTS

1) Each youth is different and will require different approaches in different situations!

2) You can only use approaches which you can adapt to your personality! If

you are not comfortable with an approach or method, the kids can see this and will use your discomfort against you!

3)   Each youth makes his or her own choices. You cannot "save" your clients. You can only help them change themselves!!! They have to make these choices for themselves!

CLASS ACTIVITIES

1)   Look at the different roles described in this book. Write a paper explaining what role you would like to take in the social service spectrum. Examine how your personality will affect how well you can do this job. Are there ways your personality will be a problem for you? How will you adapt to this environment? How realistic are these goals and on what assumptions are they based? Compare your answer to these questions now, to your answers to these same questions in chapter one? How have your answers changed?

Closing Comments

When I started to write this book I had many goals. The first was to explain the realities of a first job. The second was to give students real tools which would not only prepare them for a career working with at-risk and high-risk youths, but also make the student question whether this was the type of career they really wanted. The final reason for this book was to give youth workers in different careers a better understanding of what others do who are working with the same populations. By reading this book you have, hopefully, come to understand that everyone with whom you will work is directed by the same laws, with different expectations placed on them by these laws. Most people in the field are hard-working and want to see their clients succeed. It is our approaches and short-term goals which are different.

Good luck!

Chart 1: The Flow of Money and Authority

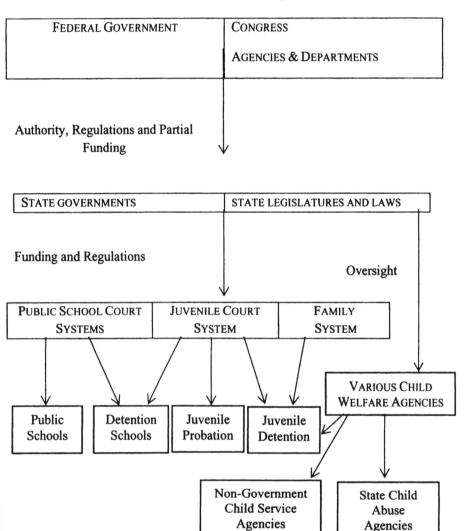

This chart illustrates how funding and regulations start at the federal level. Congress passes funding and regulatory bills. Federal agencies then interpret the laws into regulations and distribute funding down to the states. State legislatures then provide the remaining funding and additional regulations to various state agencies.

The public schools are responsible for providing education for both the general population and those youths in detention. The juvenile court system provides youths to the detention schools, directives to juvenile probation and orders youths into detention. The family court provides oversight to government agencies.

Some of these agencies provide additional oversight to the juvenile detention system. Other state agencies provide funding and oversight for state social workers, private social workers, and state and private child service agencies.

Glossary

At-Risk Youth: Any youth with a number of risk factors for future displays of socially or legally unacceptable behaviors.

Bail: Collateral posted to guarantee the appearance of a defendant at all hearings.

Case-setting: A hearing at which the parties discuss the possible ways that a case may be heard by the court and offer other options for disposition of the case.

Counselor: 1) Any person who offers advice or guidance. 2) A person working directly with a client population on an ongoing basis.

De-escalation: Methods used to remove tension from a conflict. These can include increasing personal space between the parties, speaking in a quieter tone, avoiding direct eye contact, and offering other options.

Diversion: A program to address low-risk or first-time offenders from becoming defendants within a juvenile court system.

Escalation: Methods used to increase the stress in a confrontation. These can include closing the personal space between the parties, raising the volume of the discussion, maintaining glaring eye contact, and adding additional demands onto one of the parties. Use of escalation in a confrontation should be used carefully, as the target population may be unwilling to back down.

Foster Care: Placing of a youth into a state-approved home of either a non-parental relative or a stranger.

Guardian: A person approved by the courts to act in place of a parent for a youth or non-independent adult.

Group Home: A pseudo-home environment where a population with similar needs is placed to receive services. A person's stay can be either short- or long-term.

High-Risk Youth: Any youth with a pattern of displaying socially or legally unacceptable behaviors.

Judge: A lawyer, usually appointed, who oversees the operation of the family court, the juvenile court, or both.

Juvenile Detention: A locked facility where juvenile offenders are placed for either treatment, rehabilitation, or to serve a court-imposed sentence. The nature of these institutions can include everything from long-term camps or treatment programs to permanently locked facilities where youths have limited access to each other.

Own-Recognizance: To be released before trial without having to post bail, but with specific court-imposed expectations of behavior. This is the usual status of juveniles awaiting trial for most offenses.

Parent: The legally acknowledged progenitor of a child.

Pre-trial: Abbreviation for being held pending hearings. This is the status of a juvenile who has not had bail or release conditions set. A judge may order a youth held pre-trial if the defendant has a history of not appearing, the judge considers the parents to be incapable of supervising or enabling undesirable behavior, or if the alleged crime is of enough seriousness to raise concerns about public safety if the defendant is released.

Probation Officer: A person or officer that supervises individuals who are either on pre-trial release or who have already been sentenced. This person verifies that the defendants are fulfilling their agreements, and calls the case back to court for further action if there are any questions about the defendant's actions.

Social Worker: 1) Any person who works to improve the conditions of others. 2) A state official who investigates issues of social welfare.

Teacher: 1) Any person who gives lessons to others. 2) A state official who is placed into a classroom to provide approved instruction.

Youth Program: Any ongoing activity aimed at improving youths, their environment, or their situation. These can be private, public, or governmental.

Bibliography

Arana, Ana. "How Street Gangs Took Central America." *Foreign Affairs* 84.3 (2005): doi: 845843971.

Beatty, Andrew. "How Did it Feel for You? Emotion, Narrative, and the Limits of Ethnography. *American Anthropologist* 112.3 (2010): 430-443.

Brotherton, Davis C. *Old Heads Tell Their Stories: From Street Gangs to Street Organizations in New York City.* Chicago: Spencer Foundation, 1997.

Cliford, James, and George Marcus. *Writing Culture: The Poetics and Politics of Ethnography.* Berkeley, CA: U of California P, 1986.

Cohen, David Steven, and John Eilertsen. "Folklore and Folklife in a Juvenile Corrections Institution." *Western Folklore* 44.1 (1985): 1-22.

Cottle, Thomas J. *Children in Jail: Seven Lessons in American Justice.* Boston: Beacon Press, 1977.

Cummins, Eric. *California Prison Gang Project, Final Report.* Los Gatos, CA, 1995.

Davidson, R. Theodore. *Chicano Prisoners: The Key to San Quentin.* San Francisco: Holt, 1974.

Geertz, Clifford. *The Interpretation of Culture.* New York: Harper Collins, 1973.

Huff, C. Ronald. "Comparing the Criminal Behavior of Youth Gangs and At-Risk Youths." *Alternatives to Incarceration* 5.2 (1988): 7-9.

-------. "Comparing the Criminal Behavior of Youth Gangs and At-Risk Youths." *National Institute of Justice, Research in Brief* (1988).

Hunt, Geoffrey, Karen Joe-Laidler, and Dan Waldorf. "'Drinking, Kicking Back, and Gang Banging': Alcohol, Violence and Street Gangs." *Free Inquiry in Creative Sociology* 24.2 (1996): 123-132.

Hunt, Geoffrey, Kathleen Mackenzie, and Karen Joe-Laidler. "'I'm Calling My Mom': The Meaning of Family and Kinship Among Homegirls." *Justice Quarterly* 17.1 (2000): 1-31.

Laidler, Karen Joe, and Geoffrey Hunt. "Accomplishing Femininity Among the Girls in the Gang." *The British Journal of Criminology* 41.4 (2001): 656-678.

MacLennan, Beryce W., and Naomi Felsenfeld. *Group Counseling and Psychotherapy with Adolescents.* New York: Columbia UP, 1968.

Moore, Joan, Diego Vigil, and Robert Garcia. "Residence and Territoriality in Chicago Gangs." *Social Problems* 31.2 (1983): 182-194.

Peterson, Dana, Terrance J. Taylor, and Finn-Aage Esbensen. "Gang Membership and Violent Victimization." *Justice Quarterly* 21.4 (2004): 793-815.

Pitts, John. "Describing and Defining Youth Gangs." *Community Safety Journal* 7.1 (2008): 26-32.

Plath, David W. *Long Engagements: Maturity in Modern Japan.* Stanford, CA: Stanford UP, 1980.

Powell, Colin, with Joseph E. Persico. *My American Journey.* New York: Ballantine, 1995.

Prescott, Peter. *The Children Savers: Juvenile Justice Observed.* New York: Knopf, 1981.

Reep, Beverly B. "Lessons from the Gang." *The School Administrator* 53 (1996): 26-31.

Santamaria, Carlos, Sergio Alberto Obregón, Laura Figueroa, Raul Soan, and Sergio Stern. "Estudo de una banda juvenil en una comunidad de alto riesgo: Resultados de la fase de iniciación de la relación." *Salud Mental* 12.3 (1989): 26-35.

Sobel, Russell S., and Brian J. Osoba. "Youth Gangs as Pseudo-Governments: Implications for Violent Crime." *Southern Economic Journal* 75.4 (2009): 996-1019.

Tellez, Kip, and Michelle Estep. "Latino Youth Gangs and the Meaning of School." *The High School Journal* 81.2 (1998): 69-81.

Tzu, Sun. *The Art of War.* Translated by Thomas Cleary. Boston: Shambhala Press, 1988.

Vigil, James Diego. "Chicano Gangs: One Response to Mexican Urban Adaptation in the Los Angeles Area." *Urban Anthropology* 12.1 (1983): 45-75.

-------. "Group Processes and Street Identity: Adolescent Chicano Gang Members." *Ethos* 16.4 (1988): 421-445.

15401844R00087

Made in the USA
San Bernardino, CA
23 September 2014